Mass Media Sex and Adolescent Values

To my parents,
Unice and Andrew,
for all their love
and
to my godson,
K.J. Kelvin-Eke,
because I love him

Mass Media Sex and Adolescent Values

An Annotated Bibliography and Directory of Organizations

edited by
A. Odasuo Alali

McFarland & Company, Inc., Publishers
Jefferson, North Carolina, and London

This research is funded through a Center for Population Options Research Scholarship. Conclusions and opinions are those of the author and do not necessarily reflect the views of the Center for Population Options.

British Library Cataloguing-in-Publication data are available

Library of Congress Cataloguing-in-Publication Data

Alali, A. Odasuo, 1957–
    Mass media sex and adolescent values : an annotated bibliography and directory of organizations / by A. Odasuo Alali.
        p. cm.
    Includes index.
    ISBN 0-89950-518-X (lib. bdg. : 55# alk. paper) ∞
    1. Mass media and teenagers—United States—Bibliography. 2. Sex role in mass media—United States—Bibliography. 3. Sex in mass media—United States—Bibliography. 4. Teenagers—United States—Attitudes—Bibliography. 5. Birth control—United States—Bibliography. I. Title.
    Z7164.Y8A4 1991
    [HQ799.5.M35]
    016.30223'083—dc20   91-6538
                                                          CIP

Manufactured in the United States of America

McFarland & Company, Inc., Publishers
    Box 611, Jefferson, North Carolina 28640

TABLE OF CONTENTS

Preface   **1**

1   Introduction   **5**
2   Sex-Role Portrayals   **15**
3   Sexual Curricula and Media Use   **33**
4   Adolescents' Attitudes and Values   **59**
5   Contraception, Pregnancy and Health Issues   **87**

Directory of Organizations   **103**

Suggestions for Further Reading   **125**

Index   **133**

PREFACE

The portrayal of sex in the media has increased within the past three decades. An analysis of current research findings by Louis Harris and Associates (1988) indicates that the network television affiliate stations transmitted "approximately 65,000 instances of sexual material per year just during the popular afternoon time slots (12:30–4:00 P.M.) and evening time slots (8:00–11:00 P.M.)." When this figure is examined in relation to the number of hours an average American viewer watches television, one can argue that almost 14,000 instances of sexual material would have been seen in a year. These sexual materials are not unique to drama and comedy shows, but could be seen on news shows as well.

The saturation of the media with sexual themes has not happened without protests. There are those who say that the "construction of sexual reality" in the media is responsible for lowering the sexual attitudes and morals of children. Most critics have said that the media are a source of influence for adolescent sexual behavior. Therefore, the media could be responsible for the increased incidence of sexual activity among adolescents that was widely reported in the late 1980s.

Although most media critics use nonscientific data to support their arguments, this has stimulated discussions between media institutions, nonprofit organizations, and the research community. As a result of these discussions, academic and non-academic researchers have drawn heavily on psychological and sociological theory to determine whether sexual media products

1

are hazardous to viewers such as children and adolescents. In most cases, the scientific endeavor is guided by questions such as the following: Do children and adolescents combine their developing knowledge of sex with the sexual scripts in the media? The result has been a body of literature which is somewhat paradoxical.

This book is an attempt to reflect the current research findings, discussions, articles, and analyses of mass media products and their impact, or lack of it, on adolescents' sexual attitudes, values and behavior. Although it is presented as an annotated bibliography, it is intended to illuminate the blind alleys which most researchers walk into when studying complex phenomena such as television.

The work of what eventually became this book started when I received the "An Enemy Among Us" research scholarship from the Center for Population Options in 1988. Throughout the process of identifying, editing, and compiling these entries, my colleagues and friends were very supportive. It is fitting that I express my appreciation to those who gave me the physical strength that was needed to complete this book.

Thanks are due to Kenoye Eke, Laura Fleet, Marla Iyasere, Solomon Iyasere, Beverly Kelley, and Robert Nwankwo for their continued support of my professional endeavors and quest for intellectual growth. The first draft of this manuscript was transcribed by Karen Polk. Thanks for a job well done, Karen. My research assistant, Oladejo Ibrahim, was instrumental in verifying some of the listings on research institutions and self-help organizations. This filled the void that was created by the hectic schedule most college professors are subjected to.

It would have been impossible to complete this project without the generous support of the Center for Population Options and the patience of its Studio City staff, particularly Marlene Gorland and Vanessa Poster.

I am also grateful to my brothers, Harcourt, Kenoye, Akari, Umor and Idiowa and sisters, Enighe, Ikpoki, Ilami and

Preface

Daima for their continued support. Most of my thanks, however, go to our parents, Unice and Andrew, for providing me with the opportunity to live, learn and love.

While I have tried to assemble studies which reflect adolescents and media sexuality, it is impossible to capture everything in this area. Any mistake or omission of key studies and articles is my responsibility alone.

A. Odasuo Alali
Fall 1990

3

1 INTRODUCTION

The relationship between mass media sex and adolescent values has concerned researchers for quite some time. While early experimental and field studies focused on the impact of aggressive media behavior on children, they also provided prescriptive answers which are now applied to other aspects of human interaction with the media. The one theoretical proposition that receives the most attention in media effects studies is the social learning theory. Developed by psychologist Albert Bandura, it suggests that children learn from aggressive television violence. In numerous research, Bandura and his research associates have found that television violence has a learning and motivating effect on children.

In one of his recent works on social learning theory, Bandura (1986) states that learning is a perceptual process. For example, a television viewer models or imitates behavior of a television personality known for violent acts on the basis of his or her perception of reward or punishment of the perpetrator of the violent act. While Bandura's scholarship has attracted the attention of behaviorists, other researchers have tried to conceptualize the idea that media effect is a result of integrated factors in human activity. These frameworks are now used to determine the degree to which media sex impacts on adolescents' construction of sexual reality. Although one can argue that the research activities in both academic and nonacademic communities illuminate our interpretation of how media products impact on individuals, not all research has improved our understanding of such an intricate phenomenon as the media.

Perhaps in no other aspect of the media do researchers walk into such dark alleys as they do when they attempt to analyze the role that the media play in adolescents' construction of sexual attitudes, values and behaviors. This is referred to in this book as the construction of sexual reality.

Following are operational definitions of the words "attitudes," "values" and "behaviors" as they are used in this book. Simply put, "attitudes" are consistent, learned, emotionalized predispositions to respond favorably or unfavorably to a given object, person, or situation. Accordingly, the term "is elastic enough to apply either to the dispositions of single, isolated individuals or to broad patterns of culture—common attitudes" (Allport, 1954:43).

On the other hand, "values" are our assumptions concerning good and bad, right and wrong, wise and beneficial. In short, they are deeply rooted beliefs which regulate our interactions with our environment.

Our "behaviors" are the ways we respond to certain phenomena, as conditioned by our learned predispositions and assumptions.

In view of these definitions, one might ask: Does what adolescents learn from the media intervene in their construction of sexual reality? This book is an annotated bibliography of the literature which responds to that question.

The Purpose of This Book

The purpose of this book is threefold. First, it intends to document studies and articles which reflect research findings about the relationship, or the lack of it, between adolescents' exposure to and consumption of media products and their construction of sexual reality. Secondly, this book is intended to illuminate some of the dark alleys those who have a stake in adolescent sexuality have walked into. Such persons would include parents, educators, doctors, lawyers, counselors and psychologists, law enforcement professionals and court officials, legislators, and scientists. In addition, the book will serve advanced undergraduate and graduate students in their research efforts.

Lastly, although this is an annotated bibliography, one unintended consequence is the identification of a dearth in the literature. Therefore, this undertaking should encourage other scholars to investigate issues which current researchers have ignored. In the process, our understanding of both media and the end-users of their products will be improved.

The Organization of This Book

This book is organized in a way which accommodates the threefold purpose reflected above. There are seven sections, including five numbered chapters beginning with the "Introduction." The annotated bibliography starts with Chapter 2, "Sex Role Portrayals," a compilation of studies and articles on media sex role stereotypes. Most of these studies examine how an adolescent's role identification and perceptions about sex roles at home and in the professional setting are influenced, or shaped, by media portrayals.

Sex role, as defined by Busby (1974), is "a learned association between selected attributes, behaviors, and attitudes, on one hand, and the concept male and female, on the other." The analysis of sex roles as they relate to the media is demonstrated in studies such as Drabman et al. (1981), which seeks to determine the extent to which children's perception of sex roles is influenced by media portrayals. Such analysis has led to the conclusion that "children tend to alter their perceptions or memory of a counter-stereotyped videotaped presentation to fit previously learned occupational sex stereotypes." Like most other controversial areas of study, this has not been the consensus among researchers. Other studies in this chapter reflect that paradox.

Morgan's (1987) study, for example, amplifies this contradiction by suggesting that television is not related to the actual behavior of his subjects. These findings add a feeling for the intricacies of the media and its impact on the impressionable adolescent. Additionally, the lack of consensus often associated with this inquiry has itself encouraged further analysis, which has introduced further complexity.

Chapter 2 also includes studies and articles which analyze adolescents' impressions and perceptions of the sex roles portrayed by the television actors. Some of these studies examine the impact of hero worship.

Chapter 3, "Sexual Curricula and Media Use," focuses on analyses which seek to improve a reader's understanding of the relationship between the frequency of sex in the media, adolescent media use, and adolescent social learning and sexual development. The chapter begins with Avery's (1979) analysis of adolescents' use of the media. In this study, the author suggests that teenagers are becoming increasingly tolerant of sexual contents in the media. Because of this trend, a slight correlation between the amount of television watched and sexual knowledge and attitudes of adolescents was established in studies such as that of Peterson, Moore and Furstenberg (1984). This chapter does conclude with two key research findings. The first is Van Hoose's (1980) analysis of the impact of television use on the emerging adolescent and the second finding is an essay on the historical trends in research on children and the media, from 1900 to 1960 (Wartella and Reeves, 1985).

The reader introduced to Chapter 4, "Adolescents' Attitudes and Values," would become acquainted with numerous studies analyzing how sexual media contents influence adolescents. This issue is captured in studies such as Baran's (1976) analysis of how television and film portrayals affect sexual satisfaction in college students. According to the findings of this research, sexual media messages appear to contribute to an individual's perception of his or her sexuality.

The last two chapters examine issues seldom discussed in most annotated bibliographies. Studies and articles regarding "Contraception, Pregnancy and Health Issues" constitute Chapter 5. Basically, the reader of this chapter will become familiar with adolescents' knowledge, attitudes and beliefs about contraception, pregnancy and sexually transmitted diseases (STD). Most of the studies place emphasis on various media forms, the information campaigns that are often used, and adolescents' knowledge and beliefs about STDs such as Acquired Immune Deficiency Syndrome (AIDS). The findings of these studies suggest that adolescents ignore or are unaware of the consequences of unprotected sexual behavior. Because they do not seek out such information, they put themselves and those who come in contact with them at risk.

The next section of this book, Chapter 6, is a selective "Directory of Organizations." Those who have a stake in adolescent development would find this chapter useful. A majority of the listings include nonprofit organizations that offer workshops, seminars and technical assistance to the academic and non-academic communities. The intention is to create a marketplace of ideas for those who must deal with adolescent issues and problems on a daily basis.

The reader must be cautioned that this section, and in fact the listings in the entire book, should not be regarded as inclusive of all studies, articles, research institutions and self-help organizations. A periodic update of the listings would be necessary to accommodate any omissions or new research findings.

At the end of the book, just before the index, are several pages of "Suggestions for Further Reading," divided by format. These are titles considered by the editor to be useful, to varying degrees, to persons conducting research in any aspect of this field.

Sources of Entries

In compiling these entries, the author consulted numerous scholarly publications. The relevant articles and studies were then summarized for inclusion in this volume. To facilitate this process, a computer search of the Educational Resources Information (ERIC), the National Technical Information Service (NTIS), *Psychological Abstracts, Sociological Abstracts, Social SciSearch,* and *Magazine Index* was undertaken. This was augmented by a manual search of journals and periodicals on mass media, adolescence development and sex research. Additionally, entries from the *Dissertation Abstracts International* (DAI) and *Thesis Abstracts* were useful to the completion of this work.

Conclusion

While these listings indicate some of society's efforts to generate knowledge on this subject, we must be reminded that the impact of sexual media content will not be fully understood until certain issues are reconciled between the academic and nonacademic communities. The most prominent of these issues is the obstacles which researchers confront everyday. Most researchers have indicated that they face insurmountable hurdles when studying how adolescents' relationships with the media affect their sexual behavior. This issue was the focus of discussion on the last day of a conference on "Teens, TV and Sex" organized by the Center for Population Options in Los Angeles, July 7–8, 1990. All of the discussants agreed that the three major factors which contribute to these obstacles are parents, the difficulty in ascertaining the impact of sexual scripts, and the lack of research evidence. Let us examine each of these factors.

First, researchers say they are unable to study adolescents because of their inability to secure parental consent. This age-old problem results from the reluctance of most parents to allow their children to be used as subjects for studies on sexual attitudes, values and behaviors. In most of the cases, parents tend to be up-in-arms about the researcher's intentions; what questions their children would be asked; and the consequences of such questions to their sexual attitudes, values and behaviors. Above all, most parents would prefer that no "strangers" talk to their children about sex or their attitudes. It is possible that researchers can mitigate this problem by educating parents on the scope of their research and establish the ground rules for the study.

Second, it is difficult for most researchers to ascertain whether the construction of sexual reality during adolescence comes from the media or personal experience. Consequently, when the dilemma between the construction of sexual reality and parental consent are juxtaposed, a third factor develops. That is, sufficient evidence does not exist to support or deny that the sexual reality of adolescents comes from their real life experiences or from the media products they consume.

All of these factors exacerbate the current debate on the role of the media in adolescent sexuality.

Recommendations

While parents and other organizations should play a prominent role in resolving some of the issues discussed here, researchers and media producers are the crucial determinants of how these roles are executed. Because an inevitably political policing of the industry is unnecessary, unworkable and a waste of resources, media producers should begin to consider the fragility of children and adolescents during the scripting process. They should be guided by Plato's warning about storytellers in the *Republic:*

> Children cannot distinguish between what is allegory and what is not, and opinions formed at that age are usually difficult to eradicate or change: it is therefore of the utmost importance that the first stories they hear shall aim at producing the right moral effect.

Even though this does not mean that producers should eliminate the sexual contents of their shows, their scripts need not portray sex as a commodity that the viewer can buy or sell. The entertainment value of such contents would not be lost if sex is treated in a responsible manner.

Lastly, the onus of this issue also rests with researchers. Those who study this issue must realize that adolescents are not a uniform audience for the mass media. Researchers should explore qualitative types of research into not only middle class adolescents, but also the entire ethnic diversity of the mass media audience. Is the construction of sexual reality by the African-American, Hispanic, or Native American adolescent influenced by the media? While previous studies have shown that ethnicity is a key determinant of the amount of time an adolescent spends with the media, researchers have not adequately discussed the comparative impact it has on these groups.

It is also important that the advent of music videos be examined or analyzed by researchers. Because of the sexual content of music videos, this genre of programs might have new kinds of impact which would remain cloudy if not analyzed. We must begin to ascertain whether music videos are a profound part of the socialization process of adolescents.

In view of these issues, the interpretations that researchers assigned to their findings should be humanized so as to provide others the information they need to mediate adolescents' sexual learning and to prepare them to confront real life situations. In other words, the clarification of research lingo would facilitate the mediation process for those who have a stake in adolescent development. More importantly, we must not continue to expect the media to shoulder all of the burden. Although the media, especially television, is a tube of plenty, it should only be seen as a facilitator of the developmental agenda society proposes for adolescents. We must not depend solely on the media to raise our children.

References

Allport, Gordon W. (1954). "The Historical Background of Modern Social Psychology," in Gardner Lindzey, ed., *Handbook of Social Psychology, Vol. I.* Reading, Mass.: Addison-Wesley.

Avery, Robert K. (1979). "Adolescents' Use of the Mass Media," *American Behavioral Scientist,* Vol. 23, No. 1, (September-October), pp. 53–70.

Bandura, Albert (1986). *Social Foundations of Thought and Action: A Social Cognitive Theory.* Englewood Cliffs, N.J.: Prentice Hall.

Baran, Stanley L. (1976). "How TV and Film Portrayals Affect Sexual Satisfaction in College Students," *Journalism Quarterly,* Vol. 53, No. 3 (Autumn), pp. 468–473.

Busby, Linda J. (1974). "Defining the Sex-Role Standard in Network Children's Programs," *Journalism Quarterly,* Vol. 51, No. 4 (Autumn), pp. 690–696.

Drabman, Ronald S., Stephen J. Robertson, Jana N. Patterson, Gregory J. Jarvie, David Hammer and Glenn Cordua (1981). "Children's Perception of Media-Portrayed Sex Roles," *Sex Roles,* 7(4), pp. 379–389.

Louis Harris and Associates, Inc. (1988). *Sexual Material on American Network Television During the 1987–88 Season.* New York: Planned Parenthood Federation of America, January 26.

Morgan, Michael (1987). "Television, Sex-Role Attitudes, and Sex-Role Behavior," *Journal of Early Adolescence,* Vol. 7, No. 3, pp. 269–282.

Peterson, J., K.A. Moore, and F.F. Furstenberg (1984). "Television Viewing and Early Initiation of Sexual Intercourse: Is There a Link?" (Paper presented at the American Psychological Association Meeting in Toronto, Canada, August 26).

Van Hoose, John H. (1980). "The Impact of Television Usage on Emerging Adolescents," *High School Journal,* vol. 63, No. 6 (March), pp. 239–243.

Wartella, Ellen and Byron Reeves (1985). "Historical Trends in Research on Children and the Media: 1900–1960." *Journal of Communication,* Vol. 35:2 (Spring), pp. 118–133.

2 SEX-ROLE PORTRAYALS

1 "Adolescent Sexuality and the Media" (1987). *The Facts.* Washington, D.C.: Center for Population Options (January). See annotation in Entry 120.

2 Baran, Stanley J. (1976). "Sex on TV and Adolescent Self-Image," *Journal of Broadcasting,* 20:61–8, pp. 61–68.
> The author uses high school students to determine adolescent perceptions of reality about television portrayal of sexual behavior, and its effect on their coital experience. This study amplifies the impact of television sex roles on adolescents' learned sex-role behavior.
> See more detailed annotation in Entry 121.

3 Barcus, F. Earle (1983). *Images of Life on Children's Television.* New York: Praeger Publishers.
> The analysis in this text accentuates the dominance of males in the typical television hour. Sex role portrayals depict women in either domestic or non-sophisticated domestic roles. This is in contrast to their male counterparts, who are generally depicted as important figures.

4 Barrow, Austin E., Barbara J. O'Keefe, David L. Swanson, Renee A. Meyers and Mary A. Murphy (1988). "Person

Perception and Children Impression of Television and Real Peers," *Communication Research,* Vol. 15, No. 6, pp. 680–698. Of the 126 students interviewed for this study, 119 provided the authors with usable data that measure the common processes underlying the formation of impressions of television characters and real life persons by children. The conclusion here is that children's understanding of television is based on a common set of perceptual dimensions which have implications for understanding the influence of television viewing on children. This finding is useful in the analysis of issues that pertain to media, sexuality and adolescents.

5   Busby, Linda J. (1975). "Sex-Role Research on the Mass Media," *Journal of Communication,* 25(4), pp. 107–131.
This is a comprehensive study which documents the current trends in television and print media sex-role research.

6   Busby, Linda J. (1974). "Defining the Sex-role Standard in Network Children's Programs," *Journalism Quarterly,* 51(4), pp. 690–696.
Busby explores the definitional issues of sex-role in this article. Using Jorome Kagan's definition, sex-role is presented as "...a learned association between selected attributes, behaviors, and attitudes, on one hand, and the concepts male and female, on the other."

7   Courtney, Alice E., and Thomas W. Whipple. (1983). *Sex Stereotyping in Advertising.* Lexington, Mass.: Lexington Books.
This volume reviews ten years of television commercial content which emphasizes the image of men,

women, and children. The conclusions drawn from these analyses show that sex stereotyping of these groups still exists. However, it also shows that an insignificant amount of improvement has been made.

8   Dambrot, Faye H., Diana C. Reep and Daniel Bell (1988). "Television Sex Roles in the 1980s: Do Viewers' Sex and Sex Role Orientation Change the Picture?" *Sex Roles,* Vol. 42, pp. 35–42.

The sample for this study comprises four one-hour dramas with plots that focus on crime detection, and feature a female and male sharing the leading roles as partners in a working relationship. These shows constitute part of the programs for the 1986–1987 television season. The authors' analysis of the data collected suggests the following: viewer perceptions of television characters on crime action programs are affected by their sex and sex-role orientation; viewer ratings did match the descriptions of television critics; viewers ascribe masculine traits to both female and male characters; and all the male television characters showed a pattern of low expressive traits, high instrumental traits and high stereotypical masculine behaviors.

9   Dohrmann, Rita (1975). "A Gender Profile of Children's Educational TV," *Journal of Communication,* 25(4), pp. 56–65.

This study is an analysis of sex and occupational roles depicted in four programs, *Sesame Street, The Electric Company, Mister Roger's Neighborhood,* and *Captain Kangaroo.* The author notes that the stereotypical roles in these programs confirm the societal perceptions of roles that males or females should play in America. The central issue addressed by the study is: to what extent do these stereotypical portrayals impact on the adolescents' sex roles, their choice of occupation and construction of social reality?

10 Drabman, Ronald S., Stephen J. Robertson, Jana N. Patterson, Gregory J. Jarvie, David Hammer and Glenn Cordua (1981). "Children's Perception of Media-Portrayed Sex Roles," *Sex Roles,* 7(4), pp. 379–389.

The sample for this study comprises one first-grade class, one fourth-grade class and two seventh-grade classes. The authors analyzed their impressions of sex role beliefs after they were exposed to a brief color video of a male and female doctor's interaction in 1981. In the first experiment, the data revealed that the first and fourth graders did not choose stereotyped gender names. Seventh graders appear to choose names that are associated with characters but not gender. In a second experiment, stereotype gender names were chosen for both characters by the first graders and fourth graders. Seventh graders, however, choose correct gender names for both characters. When the data were analyzed in relation to grade level following a third experiment, the result indicated that white children chose the male as doctor and the female as nurse in a ratio of 23:2. As a result of these three experiments, the authors conclude that "children tend to alter their perceptions or memory of a counterstereotyped videotaped presentation to fit previously learned occupational sex stereotypes."

11 Durall, Jean A. (1978). "Adolescent Involvement with Television Characters and Differential Attribution Strategies." (Microfiche). The University of Wisconsin–Madison, 242pp.

This is an exploratory study which documents adolescent involvement with television characters, hero worship, and television character behavior.

12   Faber, R.J., J.D. Brown, and J.M. McLeod (1979). "Coming of Age in the Global Village: Television and Adolescence." In E. Wartella (ed.), *Children Communication: Media and Development of Thought, Speech, Understanding.* Beverly Hills, Calif.: SAGE Publications.

This essay utilizes Erickson's model of developmental task resolution strategies for successful adolescent development to analyze the impact of media on adolescents. The author contends that during the adolescent stage of the life cycle, decision making strategies are developed to deal with life tasks. The choice of strategies made by the adolescent, the authors argue, is affected by the specific media content. These strategies are achievement, moratorium, foreclosure and diffusion. They are deployed within two contexts: whether or not a commitment has been made to a task resolution; and whether the individual is involved in a task crisis. The type of strategy used is affected by a number of sociocultural variables, such as the content of a television program. Accordingly, the authors suggest that the portrayal of sex role alternatives and career options can affect adolescents' task resolution.

13   Friedman, Leslie J. (1977). *Sex Role Stereotyping in the Media: An Annotated Bibliography.* New York: Garland Publishing, Inc.

This volume is an annotated bibliographical reference for researchers studying sex role stereotyping in the media. It is also a work which addresses children, television and sex role stereotypes in advertising.

14   Frueh, Terry, and Paul E. McGhee (1975). "Traditional Sex Role Development and Amount of Time Spent Watching Television," *Developmental Psychology,* Vol. 11, No. 1, p. 109.

This study tests the hypothesis that "the amount of time spent watching television would be significantly related to the strength of traditional sex role development." The authors, whose subjects were 40 boys and 40 girls, found that "high amounts of television watching are clearly associated with stronger traditional sex role development."

15 "Guide to Responsible Sexual Content in Television, Films & Music," Center for Population Options (undated).

In reaction to the explicit nature of sexual messages in film, television and music, the Center presents some suggestions for the presentation of responsible sexual content in the media. The rationale here is that current portrayals provide the young viewer with inaccurate information.

16 Hansen, Christine H., and Ronald D. Hansen (1988). "How Rock Music Videos Can Change What Is Seen When Boy Meets Girl: Priming Stereotypical Appraisal of Social Interactions," *Sex Roles,* Vol. 19, Nos. 5/6, pp. 287–316.

The authors' analysis of their subjects' reaction to music videos indicates that "stereotypic rock music videos increased the accessibility of sex role stereotypic schemas, dramatically changing impressions of the interactants."

17 Himmelweit, Hilde T., and Norma Bell (1980). "Television as a Sphere of Influence on the Child's Learning about Sexuality," in Elizabath J. Roberts (ed.), *Childhood Sexual Learning: The Unwritten Curriculum*. Cambridge, Mass.: Ballinger Publishing Company, pp. 113–137.

The authors, in part, suggest that television offers a stereotypical picture of sex roles, even though it has the potential to provide important learning about sex roles and relations.

See more detailed annotation in Entry 72.

18   Johnson, D.K., and K. Satow (1978). "Getting Down to Specifics About Sex on Television," *Broadcasting,* May 22, p. 24.

This is a survey conducted by the authors to determine the perceptions of viewers about the amount and frequency of sex on television. The initial survey elicited the following response: 78 percent of the women and 64 percent of the men said there was too much sex on television. Also, 79 percent and 68 percent, respectively, indicated that television advertisements contain too much sex. However, the women who thought there was too much sex on television said they enjoy watching soap operas. This contradictory element of the findings prompted the formation of discussion groups. In analyzing the groups' discussions, the researchers found that women, in general, do not object to sex on television per se; they object to the wrong kind of sex. For example, most of the women said they felt that sex on television is acceptable only when it is portrayed as follows: when it is implicit rather than explicit; if it is shown in a normal context; and when the viewer is prepared for it. As far as advertisements were concerned, they said they object to ads which used sexual innuendo, male fantasies, immorality, and irrelevant sex to market a product. However, sex in ads for perfumes—a commodity which has an inherent element of sexuality—was deemed acceptable.

19   "Kids and TV: What the Research Shows" (1989). In *Talking with TV: A Guide for Grown-Ups and Kids.* Washington, D.C.: Center for Population Options, pp. 5–6.

See annotation in Entry 158.

20 Lauer, Rachel M. (1988). "Evaluating Sex in Advertising," *The Humanist,* May/June, pp. 25–26.

This study evaluates an intimate perfume commercial and the sexual imagery it conveys. The author found that the classifications of imagery, following exposure to advertisements, are distinguishable. These classifications include, but are not limited to, egocentric reaction—the appealing sense of sexual satisfaction from messages that are sexually implicit.

21 Lopate, Carol (1976). "Daytime Television: You'll Never Want to Leave Home," *Feminist Studies,* 3(3/4), pp. 69–82.

This is a content analysis of randomly selected daytime television programs during the 1970s. The author designed this study to determine how daytime television programming suits the various psychological needs of women throughout the average course of a homemaker's day. The study found that in game shows and soap operas sexual and social roles for men and women are portrayed either realistically, unrealistically or idealistically. For example, the theme of "symbolic incest" is commonly identified in soaps as is a "hard-line" against any form of communication that might break down the family network. "Child-like sexuality" can also be seen in game show relationships, as "infantilized" relations between various family members on soaps, signaling that "there's no place like home" for anyone.

22 Louis Harris and Associates, Inc. (1988). *Sexual Material on American Network Television During the 1987–88 Season.* New York: Planned Parenthood Federation of America, Inc., January 26.

This comprehensive study measures the number and frequency of sexually oriented messages on television during the 1987–88 television season. It also tracks changes in the sexual content of programs over time and measures the frequency of commercial advertisements and public service announcements for contraceptives and birth control. The authors analyzed 129 videotaped television shows totaling 232 half-hour segments. The major findings are summarized as follows: over 27 instances per hour of sexual behavior were portrayed during this season; no references were made to sex education, sexually transmitted diseases, birth control, or abortion to counterbalance the sexual content on television; afternoon television contains almost 50 percent more sexual content than does evening; references to intercourse occur most frequently on night-time serial dramas. Based on these findings, the authors conclude that "over time, the number of more direct sexual references has increased, while the number of less direct types of sexual references has declined." Moreover, no commercial or public service announcement for contraceptive or birth control was aired during the period analyzed.

23   McGhee, Paul E., and Terry Frueh (1980). "Television Viewing and the Learning of Sex-Role Stereotypes," *Sex Roles,* Vol. 6, No. 2, pp. 179–188.

Departing from the traditional research on media and children, which focuses on aggressive behavior, the author determined whether a relationship exists between "the amount of time children spend watching television and their knowledge of adult sex-role stereotypes." This study found that heavy viewers tend to "have more stereotyped perceptions than light viewers."

24 Meyer, Buf (1980). "The Development of Girls' Sex-Role Attitudes," *Child Development,* 51, pp. 508–514.

The data for this study are from a representative sample of 150 girls, ages 6 to 8 and 10 to 12, from working class families in a rural Ohio town. The principal objective of this study is to determine the perceptions young girls have about adult female roles. The following variables, types of maternal influence, societal stereotypes, and age, were manipulated to determine their effect on sex-role attitudes of the sample. A questionnaire was sent to the mothers of the girls so as to determine their sex-role attitudes. The data collected revealed that the younger girls had more stereotypical sex-role attitudes than the older girls. This study also shows that the sex-role attitudes of the older girls had a significant correlation with their mothers' attitudes. The occupation of the mother had no effect on the attitudes and aspirations of their daughters.

25 Meyer, Manfred, and Nissen, Ursula (1979). *Effects and Functions of Television: Children and Adolescents; A Bibliography of Selected Research Literature, 1970–78.* Communication Research and Broadcasting Series, No. 2. New York: K.G. Saur Publishing, Inc. 172pp.

The bibliography listings in this book are useful for identifying studies which pertain to the relationship between adolescents, television and sex-role contents.

See more detailed annotation in Entry 162.

26 Miles, Beth (1975). *Channeling Children: Sex Stereotyping in Prime-Time TV.* Princeton, N.J.: Women on Words and Images.

In this study, the author argues that sex role portrayals during the prime-time hours of television constitute displays of "competent" behavior which are easily adopted by those who watch it, especially children. As a result, the stereotypical sex-role portrayals on television are often channeled to children.

27   Morgan, Michael (1987). "Television, Sex-Role Attitudes, and Sex-Role Behavior," *Journal of Early Adolescence,* Vol. 7, No. 3, pp. 269–282.

This study measures the amount of television viewing, sex-role attitudes, and sex-role behavior of 287 adolescents. The data analyzed suggest that television viewing makes an independent contribution to adolescents' sex-role attitudes over time, but is not, however, related to their actual behavior. Additionally, there is documentation to support the contention that a relationship which exists between viewing and attitude is mediated by behavior. The study suggests that a reciprocal relationship exists between the amount of viewing and the degree of congruence between sex-role attitudes and behavior.

28   Morgan, Michael Jay (1980). "Longitudinal Patterns of Television Viewing and Adolescent Role Socialization." (Ph.D. Dissertation, University of Pennsylvania, 298pp.)

In this analysis of the patterns of television viewing and adolescent role socialization, the study suggests that television has an independent positive impact on the extent to which girls endorse sex-role stereotypes. Based on the data the author analyzed, the study concludes that girls who watch more television in early adolescence are more likely to believe in later adolescence that women are happiest at home raising children and that men have more ambition than women.

29   O'Kelly, Charlotte G. (1974). "Sexism in Children's Television," *Journalism Quarterly,* 51(4), pp. 722–724.

Using seven hours of children's television shows for analysis, the author concluded that sexism is disproportionately displayed in favor of young boys than young girls. Females were depicted more in "traditional" female and low authority jobs such as housewife and mother.

30   Ornelas, Kriemhild Conee (1987). "The Depiction of Sexuality in Daytime Television Melodrama." (Ph.D. Dissertation, Bowling Green State University, 255pp.)

Over 30 consecutive broadcasts of three popular soap operas — "Days of Our Lives," "The Young and Restless," and "General Hospital" — composing a sample of 90 viewing hours were analyzed. The manner in which sex-related behaviors and verbal references occur in the daytime soap serials are documented in this study.

31   Signorielli, Nancy (1985). *Role Portrayal and Stereotyping on Television: An Annotated Bibliography of Studies Relating to Women, Minorities, Aging, Sexual Behavior, Health, and Handicaps.* Westport, Conn.: Greenwood Press.

This is a comprehensive annotated bibliography which includes current research on sex-roles and role portrayals on television.

32   Silverman, L. Theresa, Joyce N. Sprafkin, and Eli Rubinstein (1979). "Physical Contact and Sexual Behavior on Prime-Time TV," *Journal of Communication,* 29(1), pp. 33–43.

The analysis of regularly scheduled prime-time television programs for one week in the 1977–78 season indicated that even though females constituted 32 percent of the 678 characters identified in this study, they were more likely to be cast in roles which engage in sexual behavior and innuendos, such as hugging, kissing, and affectionate touching. For example, flirtatious behavior was recorded at a rate of 3.26 times per hour.

33 Simon, Rogers (1987). "Casual Sex on TV: Part of the Problem," *Los Angeles Times,* January 4.

This article documents studies which suggest that attitudes about sex and birth control won't change without changes on television. In support of this argument, the author notes that even though sex is open on television today, birth control is still viewed as a deep, dark secret. The basic contention here is that because television is part of the problem, the issue of responsible sexuality can not be reconciled if television is not part of the solution.

34 Sprafkin, Joyce N., and L. Theresa Silverman (1981). "Update: Physically Intimate and Sexual Behavior on Prime-Time Television, 1978–79," *Journal of Communications,* 31(1), pp. 34–40.

This is an update of an earlier study on the types of sexual behavior exhibited on television. Using 68 programs, representative of the prime-time (8 P.M. to 11 P.M.) 1978–79 season recorded over a two-week period, the authors analyzed the contents to determine the frequency of sexual and intimate behavior on television. The data collected suggest that 10 times the number of sexual innuendos and 25 times the number of both implied and verbal references to intercourse were found in the 1978–79 television season, as compared to three years ago. The frequency of appearance of the least intimate behaviors (kissing and hugging) showed a gradual increase over

the three years sampled. Contextually implied intercourse increased from none in 1975 to 15 in 1977, and
24 in 1978. Direct verbal references to intercourse
dramatically increased from 2 occurrences per week
in 1975 to 6 in 1977, and 53 in 1978. Allusions to prostitution increased more than four times, and allusions to aggressive sexual contacts increased three
times from 1977 to 1978. As was found in the 1977
analysis, socially-disapproved sexual practices in
1978 were more frequently referred to between 9 P.M.
and 11 P.M. (5.06 acts per hour) than between 8 P.M.
and 9 P.M. (.48 acts per hour). Situation comedies
tended to handle this type of material, where crime/
adventure programs dealt more with aggressive sexual behaviors, and dramas tended to deal more with
prostitution. Dramas and movies, however, presented substantially more direct references to intercourse and socially discouraged practices such as
prostitution and rape.

35   Sprafkin, Joyce N., L. Theresa Silverman, and Eli A.
Rubinstein (1980). "Reaction to Sex on Television: An Exploratory Study," *Public Opinion Quarterly,* 44(3), Fall, pp.
303–315.

A total of 660 adults watched one of 15 half-hour
or hour shows randomly selected from prime-time
network programming in the fall of 1977 to determine the degree of physical intimate and sexual content of these programs. The contents were then rated
for its suitability for viewing by children, teenagers,
and adults. The subjective ratings given by the adults
seem to relate intercourse with the objectively coded
instances of affectionate touching, suggestiveness,
kissing, prostitution, and other sexual behavior. As
such, intercourse is much more frequent than the

trained observers' rating showed. In terms of viewer suitability, the adults' ratings were inversely correlated with the amount of kissing, affectionate touching, suggestiveness, prostitution, and other atypical sexual behavior. For teenage audiences, the respondents gave a mixed verdict. Several of the topics, including birth control, abortion, petting, and marital sex, were rated as having been presented in a suitable fashion by the majority of those surveyed. Only portrayals of child molestation, rape and homosexuality were thought to have been presented unsuitably for adult audiences by a significant proportion of the survey group. In conclusion, the study argues that 91 percent of the group felt that there was too much violence on television, compared to the 61 percent who felt that there was too much sex. Forty-eight percent felt that exposure to television violence is worse than exposure to sex, and only 3 percent felt the reverse was true. However, 44 percent felt that sex and violence were equally bad.

36 Sternglaz, Sarah Hall, and Lias A. Serbin (1974). "Sex-role Stereotyping in Children's Television Programs," *Developmental Psychology,* 10(5), pp. 710–715.

In an analysis of male and female role models presented on 10 popular commercially produced children's television programs, the authors found "striking sex differences in the number of male and female roles portrayed and the behaviors which were emitted by the characters." This study also discusses the implication for stereotyped sex role development of children.

37 Stillion, Judith M., and Eugene E. McDowell (1983). "The Influence of a Multi-Media Presentation on Sex-Role

Stereotyping in Gifted Adolescents." Paper presented at the Annual Meeting of the Southeastern Psychological Association (29th, Atlanta, March 23–26). 9pp. (ED 235-405.)

To determine the effectiveness of a short, intense teaching session on sex role attitudes of adolescents, 51 gifted ninth- and tenth-grade students participated in a 3-hour workshop. The findings suggest that brief modules of formal instruction by male and female teachers are ineffective in reducing sex role stereotyping among gifted adolescents.

38   Streenland, Sally (1989). "TV Still Struggling with Teenage Reality." *Media & Values,* (Spring) 46:19.

This article examines ways which television sitcoms, such as "A Different World," "Head of the Class," and "Mr. Belvedere," present sexual behavior. The author argues that "Although TV is far from perfect in its treatment of adolescent sexuality, it offers more authenticity and equality among sexes, young and old, than there was decades ago."

39   Tan, Alexis S. (1979). "TV Beauty Ads and Role Expectations of Adolescent Female Viewers," *Journalism Quarterly,* 56, pp. 283–288.

The sample for this study comprised 56 high school girls, ages 16 to 18, who were divided into two groups: One group was exposed to beauty commercials depicting sex appeals and the second set of subjects were exposed to commercials that did not have a sexual implication or theme. Both sets of commercials were taped approximately one month before the actual study. Both subjects watched 15 minutes of commercials. The subjects were then given a list of questions about the importance of beauty characteristics. The subjects exposed to beauty commercials rated beauty characteristics a higher order of importance than those who watched the neutral commercials.

40   Uselding, Douglas K. (1979). "Assessing the Level of Sex-Role Stereotyping on Children's Preferred Programming." *Technical Report No. 1: Children's Use of Television as a Source of Social Role Models.* University of South Dakota, Department of Psychology.

This analysis focuses on 64 TV programs comprising of 174 leading characters. Stereotypes of the sexes were skewed toward the female from a "traditional role" perspective. The social consequences is that it mirrors patterns of sex roles frequently shown on television.

41   "What You Don't Know About Teen Sex: How Often They Do It, How Little They Tell" (1987). *People Weekly,* April 13.

See annotation in Entry 115.

42   "What's on Tonight? TV Shows with Pre-Teen Appeal" (1989). In *Talking with TV: A Guide for Grown-Ups and Kids.* Washington, D.C.: Center for Populations Options, pp. 7–12.

See annotation in Entry 116.

3 SEXUAL CURRICULA AND MEDIA USE

43   "A New Sexuality: TV Beginning to Treat Sex as Serious Subject." (1987). *Dayton Daily News and Journal Herald,* Sunday, June 28.

> This article explores the new genre of programs which depict characters who do not only engage in sex but talk about the consequences. Specific programs are identified in the article.

44   Abramson, P.R., and M.B. Mechanic (1983). "Sex and the Media: Three Decades of Best Selling Books and Major Motion Pictures." *Archives of Sexual Behavior,* 12:3, pp. 185–206.

> While this study does not specifically address adolescents, the findings have implications on adolescent use of the media. To analyze the amount of sexual elements in the media, the authors selected the top five books and the top five films from the last years of three consecutive decades: 1959, 1969 and 1979. The contents were itemized within a 29-item scoring category and analyzed. The general conclusions are summarized as follows: the amount of sexual elements in books increased from 22 situations in 1959 to 40 and 48 in 1969 and 1979, respectively; contraceptives were absent in 90 percent of the cases. Contraceptives were absent in 100 percent of all

movies; sexual dysfunctions were identified in 50 percent of the scenes.

45   Avery, Robert K. (1979). "Adolescents' Use of the Mass Media." *American Behavioral Scientist,* Vol. 23, No. 1, September-October, pp. 53–70.

The analysis here documents adolescent development processes and uses of the mass media, including records. With a focus on adolescents aged 12–18, the study concludes that teenagers are increasingly tolerant of sexual and violent contents in the media.

46   Bandura, Albert, and Richard H. Walters (1963). *Social Learning and Personality Development.* New York: Holt, Rhinehart and Winston, 329pp.

This book is one of the early studies to document how social learning and personality development are influenced by the media. Basically, the authors posit that because American children and adolescents do not observe actual sexual behavior, they are forced to depend on the mass media for sexual learning, maturity and socialization.

47   Banks, Ivan W., and Patricia I. Wilson (1989). "Appropriate Sex Education for Black Teens." *Adolescence,* Vol. XXIV, No. 93, pp. 233–245.

This year-long study of black teens emphasizes two key issues: black teenagers' perception of the most influential family member; and dating habits, sexual behavior and attitudes toward contraception. The findings show their perceptions of the influential roles played by either their father or mother. Overall, it indicates the age most black teens start dating and when sex was first initiated. At least 22.8 percent of the boys and 55.7 percent of girls did not have birth control or contraception information. The source of their initial information on birth control includes magazines, movies, radio and television.

48   "The Birds, the Bees and Broadcasting: What the Media Teaches Our Kids About Sex" (1989). *Media & Values* (Spring), No. 4.

This special issue examines several aspects of adolescent sexuality; what the media teaches them about sex; and the consequences of sex. The articles include "Decoding MTV: Values, Views and Videos." There is also a close-up look at MTV and teen magazines.

49   Brion-Meisels, Stevens et al. (1982). *Adolescent Development and Sexuality: Adolescent Decisions Curriculum*. Boston, Mass.: Judge Baker Guidance Center. (ED 236-444), 302pp.

This is an excellent manual for educators. It examines the most crucial issues of adolescent sexuality and social relationships. Included in this package are 23 content lessons ranging from sexual activity to parenting.

50   Cantor, Muriel G., and Joel M. Cantor (1989). "Do Soaps Teach Sex?" *Media & Values*, (Spring) 46:5.

The authors' analysis of soap operas show that morality on these programs have changed over the years. Consequently, emphasis is often placed on premarital sex and adultery. Based on this analysis, the authors conclude that teenagers learn sexual manners and morals from soap operas.

51   Childers, Kim Walsh, and Jane Brown (1989). "No Blank Slate: Teen Media Awareness Mirrors Upbringing," *Media & Values*, (Spring), 46:8–10.

The authors argue that "media sex has come a long

way from the days of Ozzie and Harriett's twin beds." Today, it is noted, "couples are frequently seen in bed during daytime dramas and on late evening shows." Because adolescents watch an average of five-and-a-half to eight hours of television everyday, they are exposed to too much sex. From an analysis of data from their indepth 1987 study, the authors believe that adolescents' interpretation of media sexuality depends on each person. "More specifically, it depends on the way they look at the media and on what they've learned from their families about media sexuality." The study found three distinct categories of young viewers.

52 Csikszentmihalyi, Mihaly, et al. (1977). "The Ecology of Adolescent Activity and Experience." *Journal of Youth and Adolescence,* Vol. 6, No. 3, (September), pp. 281–294.

The adolescents who constitute the sample for this study were found to have spent most of their time conversing with peers or involved in television viewing. The implication here is that tele-viewing, for this group, is associated with deviance and antisocial personality.

53 Cullari, Salvatore, and Robert Mikus (1990). "Correlates of Adolescent Sexual Behavior," *Psychological Reports,* 66, pp. 1179–1184.

See annotation in Entry 132.

54 DiClemente, Ralph J., Jim Zorn, and Lydia Temoshok (1986). "Adolescents and AIDS: A Survey of Knowledge, Attitudes and Beliefs about AIDS in San Francisco." *American Journal of Public Health,* 76(12), pp. 1443–1445.

This article discusses adolescents knowledge, attitudes, and beliefs about AIDS in the San Francisco area. The research found, among other things, that 92 percent of the students in this survey knew that AIDS is a sexually transmitted disease.

See more detailed annotation in Entry 196.

55 Duncan, David F. (1990). "Pornography as a Source of Sex Information for University Students," *Psychological Reports,* 66, p. 442.

To determine whether pornography is a source of sex information, the author administered a questionnaire on 32 students. One of the findings indicate that pornography is a source of information about sex.

56 Ehrenberg, Mariam, and Otto Ehrenberg (1988). *The Intimate Circle: The Sexual Dynamics of Family Life.* New York: Simon & Schuster.

This book debunks the myth that sex is not a significant force in children's lives before they reach puberty. The authors argue that the early years can be the most crucial in children's sexual development and therefore parents cannot ignore children's questions about sex.

57 Eisen, Marvin, and Gail L. Zellman (1984). "Health Belief Model-Based Changes in Sexual Knowledge, Attitudes and Behavior." Paper presented as part of the Symposium: A Health Belief Model Approach to Improving Adolescent Fertility Control at the Annual Convention of the American Psychological Association (92nd, Toronto, Ontario, Canada, August 24–28), 23pp. (ED 263-499).

In this study, a Health Belief Model (HBM)-based educational intervention intended to increase adolescents' fertility control by encouraging abstinence or effective contraceptive usage was evaluated during preintervention interviews with 203 adolescents.

From the HBM perspective, the findings demonstrate substantial relationships between some health beliefs, sexual knowledge, and subsequent contraceptive usage for adolescents who were or became sexually active following the program.

See also annotation in Entry 134.

58   Fink, Mitchell (1986). "TV Gets Poor Grade in Sex Education." *Los Angeles Herald Examiner,* Sunday, June 15.

This article reflects the opinions of panelists during a seminar in Universal City. Television, the panelists argue, influences teen sexual behavior through its programs. Yet, it ignores contraception. Other issues discussed include the impact of low self-esteem and television's duty to society.

59   Finkel, Madelon L., and David J. Finkel (1975). "Sexual and Contraceptive Knowledge, Attitudes and Behavior of Male Adolescents." *Family Planning Perspectives,* 7(6), pp. 256–260.

This study is composed of 421 male students from three high schools in a large northeastern city. In analyzing the data collected, the authors found that the initial sexual activity for males begin at 12.8 years of age, although the activity remained sporadic in nature. Ninety-two percent of the respondents indicated that they used a condom always or many times. At last coitus though, only 28 percent reported using a condom. Of those respondents whose female partners used contraception, 63 percent stated that they never or seldom used a condom. The data also indicate that 30 percent of the males used withdrawal or their partners relied on douche as a means of contraception at last coitus.

60 Frueh, Terry, and Paul E. McGhee (1975). "Traditional Sex Role Development and Amount of Time Spent Watching Television," *Development Psychology,* Vol. 11, No. 1, p. 109.
See annotation in Entry 14.

61 Fuchs, Lucy (1984). "The Hidden Messages in Children's Books." Paper presented at the Annual Meeting of the Florida Reading Association (22nd, Jacksonville, Florida, October 18–21), 12pp. (ED 252-856).
This paper analyzes children's books, their portrayal of sex, birth control, and other related issues. The findings are useful for interpreting issues that revolve around the sexual learning and knowledge of those exposed to these messages.
See also annotation in Entry 144.

62 Gerbner, George (1980). "Sex on Television and What Viewers Learn from It." Comments Prepared for the National Association of Television Program Executives Annual Conference, San Francisco, Calif., February 19.
This study analyzed samples of prime-time programs broadcast between 1977 and 1978. The author concludes that "references to homosexual or bisexual behavior increased from 7 percent of the programs in 1977 to 10 percent in 1978." Additionally, the study indicates that publicly accepted sexual behavior such as kissing and embracing became more explicit and frequent during the period under analysis. This is to say that, during the period under study, "More controversial matters such as premarital and extramarital sex just became more frequent, with references to such behavior rising from 21 percent of primetime programs in 1977 to 43 percent in 1978."

63   Goldfarb, Lori, Meg Gerrard, Frederick X. Gibbens, and Thomas Plante (1988). "Attitudes Toward Sex, Arousal, and the Retention of Contraceptive Information." *Journal of Personality and Social Psychology,* Vol. 55, No. 4, pp. 634–641.

The physiological responses of erotophobic and erotophitic women who viewed presentations about contraception were monitored to determine learning and retention of sexually relevant material, such as contraception information. The result indicates that the erotophobic women knew less contraceptive information before the presentation and were more aroused by the presentation. This did not, however, interfere with the retention of the material. The results are discussed in terms of individual difference in perspective as it relates to reaction to sexual materials and the ability to learn, retain, and use contraceptive information.

64   Gore, Tipper (1987). *Raising PG Kids in an X-rated Society.* Nashville, Tenn.: Abingdon Press.

This book provides parents with guidelines on how to protect their children from explicit media messages.

65   "Guide to Responsible Sexual Content in Television, Film & Music." Center for Population Options (undated).

See annotation in Entry 15.

66   Haffner, Debra W., and Marcy Kelly (1987). "Adolescent Sexuality in the Media." *SIECUS Report,* pp. 9–12.

This study analyzes media portrayal of sexuality and its impact on adolescent sexual behavior. The report draws from television programs, radio shows, movies and advertisements to conclude that the suggestive behaviors transmitted by these mediums serve as sources of information about sexuality for teenagers. The analysis also includes two "number one" songs—"Papa Don't Preach," by Madonna, which glorifies teenage childbearing, and "Detente," by Tatiana and Johnny, which encourages the young to wait to have sexual intercourse. The explicit sexual references in book lyrics appear to impact on adolescents, their sexual attitudes and behavior, the authors concluded.

67   Haignere, Clara S. (1987). "Planned Parenthood Harris Poll Findings: Teens' Sexuality Knowledge and Beliefs." Paper Presented at the Annual Children's Defense Fund National Conference, Washington, D.C. N.Y.: Planned Parenthood Federation of America, Inc., March 11–13, 38pp. (ED 286-086).

The findings of this study are the result of a national public opinion poll conducted by Louis Harris for Planned Parenthood. The poll asked one thousand 12–17 year olds about their knowledge and beliefs on the problem of teenage pregnancy. The results show that over 50 percent of those surveyed have had sexual intercourse before their 18th birthday. The sexually active respondents indicated that social pressure, followed by curiosity and sexual gratification, were reasons for being sexually active. The majority said they use contraceptives; 40 percent had no sex education in school; only 35 percent had comprehensive sexuality education. Their sources of information include parents (although many respondents said they never discussed sexuality with their parents). Television, according to this study, gives realistic views of sexually transmitted diseases, pregnancy, the consequences of sex, and family planning.

68   Hawkins, Robert P., David H. Gustafson, Betty Chewning, Kris Bosworth, and Patricia M. Day (1987). "Reaching Hard-to-Reach Populations: Interactive Computer Programs as Public Information Campaigns for Adolescents." *Journal of Communication,* Vol. 37, No. 2, pp. 8–28.

With a sample of 5,500 adolescents from schools in the Madison, Wisconsin, area, the authors examined how learning and behavioral changes can be achieved among the hard-to-reach adolescent population. They argue that because computer programs provide certain opportunities not available in other media forms, the Body Awareness Resources Network (BARN — an interactive computer program which can be run on any Apple II computer with 64K — has the potential to provide information and can serve as a successful tool for attracting adolescents who exhibit or might have the potential to exhibit high-risk behavior such as sexuality, drugs, and cigarette smoking. In analyzing their data, it became evident that "Human Sexuality," one of the quiz games in BARN, was the most popular among adolescents.

To order BARN, see Entry 252.

69   Heffley, Lynne (1980). "Teen-Agers Share Pain in 'Taking Care.'" *Los Angeles Times,* May 3, Section VI, Column 1, p. 6.

The author reviews a musical play by and for teenagers. This play, "Taking Care," deals with sex, drugs and AIDS. It was showcased at the California Museum of Science and Industry.

70   Hein, K. (1980). "Impact of Mass Media on Adolescent Sexual Behavior." *American Journal of Disordered Child,* 13, 4:133–134.

This study analyzes the media contents and the

impact it has on the observable sexual behavior of adolescents.

71 Hendry, Leo B., and Helen Patrick (1977). "Adolescents and Television." *Journal of Youth and Adolescence,* Vol. 6, No. 4, pp. 325–336.

The sample for this study includes 15- to 16-year-old pupils attending 12 comprehensive schools in Central Scotland. A total of 2,302 subjects (1044 boys and 1258 girls) participated. With variables such as sex and viewing frequency isolated, the authors found that high frequency viewers are more likely to have lower academic attainment than low frequency viewers, but no significant social class differences were found between high and low frequency viewers; and high frequency viewers were found to be more neurotic and introverted than low frequency viewers.

72 Himmelweit, Hilde T., and Norma Bell (1980). "Television as a Sphere of Influence on the Child's Learning about Sexuality." In Elizabeth J. Roberts (ed.) *Childhood Sexual Learning: The Unwritten Curriculum.* Cambridge, Mass.: Ballinger Publishing Company, pp. 113–137.

This is a thorough analysis of television and how it facilitates the social learning of sexuality in children. The authors draw from sociological and psychological variables in relating program content to cultural values and its relationship to the individual. In the analysis of sexuality, the study notes that overt kissing, embracing, or affectionate touching are characteristics of situation comedies and they serve as helpmates for social construction of sexual "reality." Television, it is argued, offers a very stereotyped picture of sex roles and sexual behavior, even though it has the potential to provide important learning about sex roles and relations. The authors recommend the institution of a code of practice; periodic content analysis of programs; the development of programs designed to increase awareness among children and teenagers; and suggests that the Action for Children's Television, Parent Teacher Association, and other organizations should continue to monitor programs presented on television.

73   Holroyd, H.J. (1985). "Children, Adolescents, and Television." *American Journal of Disordered Children,* 139:549–550.

This study examines the relationship between television and teenagers. It concludes that the portrayals of teenagers are often distorted and over-emphasize sexuality; television has become increasingly sexual; and MTV (Music Television) is overtly sexual.

74   Horn, John (1986). "Experts Say Television Is a Factor in Teen Pregnancy Crisis," *The Orange County Register,* (Television Page), Monday, June 16.

See annotation in Entry 205.

75   "Kids and Sex: How to Make TV an Ally." (1989). In *Talking with TV: A Guide for Grown-ups and Kids.* Washington, D.C.: Center for Population Options, pp. 2–4.

This article shows how television programs can be used as springboards for discussions about adolescent sexuality and sexual behavior.

76   Kirby, Douglas, and Philip D. Harvey, David Claussenius, and Marty Novar (1989). "A Direct Mailing to Teenage Males About Condom Use: Its Impact on Knowledge, Attitudes and Sexual Behavior." *Family Planning Perspectives,* (January/February) Vol. 21, No. 1, pp. 12–18.

A letter, information/pamphlet and order coupon for free mail-order condoms were sent to an experimental group of teenage males 16–17 years of age. On this basis, the authors designed an experiment to measure the impact of the mailing on teenagers knowledge, attitudes and behavior. Results of the study indicate that the experimental group was significantly more likely to have ordered condoms by mail, presumably as a result of having received the mail-order condom offer. The findings have implication for early intervention, through direct mail techniques.

77   Levy, Joseph R. (1986). "The Daytime Soaps Examine Their Morals." *Los Angeles Herald Examiner,* (Style Section), Tuesday, October 14.

This article documents the proceedings of a seminar, "Sex and the Daytime Drama," where producers of daytime soap serials such as "The Young and Restless," "General Hospital," and "Days of Our Lives" examine the role of soaps in shaping teenage sexuality. And because producers participated in the proceedings, it serves as a looking-glass image of television. One of the discussants reported that "Media ranks third, right after parents and peers, in shaping teens' values, such as sexual values."

78   Lopez-Johnson, Pam (1989). "'Dr. Ruth' to Host Talk Show for Teen-Agers," *Los Angeles Times,* June 10, Section V, Column 3, p. 10.

This article announces the debut of Dr. Ruth Westheimer's cable–TV talk show for teenagers. Called "What's Up, Dr. Ruth?," it will provide sexual advice to teens so as to help them overcome the conflicts and questions they encounter during adolescence.

79   Luria, Zella (1982). "Sexual Fantasy and Pornography: Two Cases of Girls Brought Up with Pornography," *Archives of Sexual Behavior,* Vol. 11, No. 5, pp. 395–404.

The author interviewed two sisters whose family was involved in pornographic publishing to determine their sexual histories. The author found that repeated exposure to pornography could lead to the incorporation of the pornographic imagery into fantasy and to arousal.

80   McGhee, Paul E., and Terry Frueh (1980). "Television Viewing and the Learning of Sex-Role Stereotypes," *Sex Roles,* Vol. 6, No. 2, pp. 179–188.

See annotation in Entry 23.

81   Meyer, Manfred, and Ursula Nissan (1979). *Effects and Functions of Television: Children and Adolescents. A Bibliography of Selected Research Literature 1970–78.* (Communication Research and Broadcasting Series, No. 2). New York: Saur Publishing, Inc., 172pp.

This is a bibliography of selected research findings on subjects such as adolescents' sexual knowledge, contraception, and the role of television in these processes.

See also annotation in Entry 162.

82   Newcomer, Susan F. (1985). "Does Sexuality Education Make a Difference?" New York: Planned Parenthood Federation of America, Inc., 7pp. (ED 269-673).

Discussions in this study center on the pros and cons of sexuality education. This study, which documents the effectiveness of sexuality education among college students, suggests little relevance for teenage sexuality education. The report, which includes 15 references, shows that sexuality education did not increase the likelihood that teenagers would have sexual intercourse or that their values would change as a result of the program. This has general implications for the media because the study suggests that sexuality education can be useful in continued and improved access to contraception, and safe legal abortion, which will prevent children from having children.

83   O'Bryant, Shirley L., and Charles R. Corder-Bolz (1978). "Black Children's Learning of Work Roles from TV Commercials," *Psychological Reports,* 42: 227–230.

This study examines whether black children learn about work roles and the sex of workers in those roles from television commercials. It was found that the black child's knowledge of sex roles and occupation increased after exposure to television.

84   Okigbo, Charles (1986). "Television in the Lives of Nigerian Youths." Paper presented at the International Television Studies Conference in London, England (July 10–12) (ED 294-530).

This study is designed to determine the nature of Nigerian young people's access to and use of television and the competing media of radio and newspapers, their television station preferences, and choice of specific programs. The analysis of usable data indicates that television preoccupies the lives of adolescents, a finding consistent with earlier research in this area.

85   Padgett, Vernon R., Jo Ann Brislin-Slutz, and James A. Neal (1989). "Pornography, Erotica, and Attitudes Toward

Women: The Effects of Repeated Exposure," *The Journal of Sex Research,* Vol. 26, No. 4, pp. 479–491.
See annotation in Entry 168.

86   Peterson, J., K.A. Moore, and F.F. Furstenberg (1984). "Television Viewing and Early Initiation of Sexual Intercourse: Is There a Link?" Paper presented at the American Psychological Association Meeting in Toronto, Canada, August 26.

This longitudinal survey completed in 1981 establishes only a slight correlation between the amount of television watched and sexual learning, knowledge and attitudes of subjects.

87   Peterson, R., and Kahn, J. (1984). "Media Preferences of Sexually Active Teens: A Preliminary Analysis." Presented at the American Psychological Association Meeting in Toronto, Canada, August 26.

This study is an analysis of a 1983 survey of teenagers in Cleveland, Ohio. The authors argue that "a preference for MTV and other music television programs is associated with increased sexual experience among 14–16 year olds." Whether or not the implication of this study goes far beyond Cleveland is an issue of analytical concern.

88   Planned Parenthood Federation of America, Inc. (1982). *Sexuality Education Can Make a Difference. Reference Sheet 1 and Bibliography of Selected Resources.* New York, N.Y.: 14pp. (ED 271-644).

Thirty-five citations from 1970 to the early 1980s cover topics on teenage pregnancy, sexuality and adolescents, family life and sexuality education, contraception, adolescent development, and human sexuality.

48

89   Planned Parenthood Federation of America, Inc. (1986). *Teen Sexuality Today: Bibliography of Selected Resources.* New York, N.Y.: 27pp. (ED 296-201).

This document is a selected bibliography of recent publications relating to adolescent sexuality and reproduction health. The 11 books and 102 journal articles that comprise this document are divided into nine areas: sexuality education, contraception, parenthood, communication with parents, reproduction health, sexual behavior, school-based programs, teenage life in general, and male involvement.

90   Price, James H. (1978). "Television-Health Education or Mental Pollution?" *Health Education,* Vol. 9, pp. 24-26 (March-April).

The author examines the types of ideas television programs and commercials communicate. The study concludes that inaccurate ideas are usually presented about family life, health products, nutrition and sex. Suggestions for improvements are offered.

91   "Puppets Get Kids Talking" (1988). *Options,* Vol. 1, Issue 1 (Spring), p. 7.

This article examines the use of large-scale puppets to give teens the opportunity to ask questions about difficult issues, such as sex. Interested parties should call Barbara Aiello at 1-800-368-KIDS.

92   Puttman, David (1988). "Film Makers Are Missing Their Social Purpose," *Los Angeles Times,* May 2, Section II, Column 1, p. 7.

This author's commentary on the social role of filmmakers argues that they have undeniable formative influence over younger viewers. As a result, the author argues that the future lies in the hands of those who make films and television shows.

93   Raksin, Alex (1988). "Nonfiction in Brief," *Los Angeles Times,* January 24, Section B, Column 2, p. 4.

In this article, the author reviews a book entitled *The Intimate Circle: The Sexual Dynamics of Family Life,* by Mariam and Otto Ehrenberg. The book discusses the importance of addressing children's sexuality before puberty.

94   Rensberger, Boyce (1978). "Behavioral Study Indicates Many Parents Don't Tell Children of Erotic Aspects of Sex." *New York Times,* December 17, p. 30.

This article analyzes a study that was conducted in Cleveland, Ohio. It documents interesting findings about parents' attitudes when it comes to sexual education. The study found that very few of the parents (less than 15 percent of the mothers, 8 percent of the fathers) had talked about sexual intercourse with their children. Even fewer mentioned anything about birth control or venereal disease. The parents stated that they failed to talk about sex because they were worried about transmitting their own attitudes and values to their children. Eighty percent of the parents said that sex education should be taught in the school. Sixty-two percent said that pre-teenagers ought to have information about contraception. The director of the project said that parents are not talking about sex at all. They are waiting for their children to ask them, but the children get the nonverbal message that sex is a forbidden subject.

95   Rifkin, Ira (1989). "Sex and Consequences: Reflections of a TV Writer," *Media & Values* (Spring) 46:6–7.

This essay is an interview with Dan Wakefield, creator of "James at 15," the innovative and critically acclaimed 1977–78 NBC series. The series, which was cancelled, pioneered the realistic treatment of teen-age sexuality in the late 70s.

96   Roberts, E., D. Kline, and J. Gagnon (1978). *Family Life and Sexual Learning: A Study of the Role of Parents in the Sexual Learning of Children.* N.p.: Population Education.

Although this study discusses the role parents play in the sexual learning of their children, it has implications for the media. When the authors surveyed 1,400 Cleveland parents to determine their roles, it was found that television was the highest ranked source (after the parents themselves) of sexual learning for their children and, in particular, a source of inaccurate information about sex.

97   Roberts, Elizabeth J. (1982). "Television and Sexual Learning in Childhood." In David Pearl, Lorraine Bonthilet, and Loyce Lazar (eds.). *Television and Behavior: Ten Years of Scientific Progress and Implications for the Eighties.* Washington, D.C.: GPO, pp. 209–223.

This study analyzes how television programs impact on sexual learning and performance during childhood. Most programs emphasize sex, the author argues. This can impact on childhood learning about sexuality.

98   Rubin, Alan M. (1979). "Television Use by Children and Adolescents." *Human Communication Research* (Winter), Vol. 5, No. 2, pp. 109–120.

This study examines the relationship between child and adolescent television viewing motivation and sociodemographic variables. The study has implications within the uses-and-gratification research perspective.

99 Sanders, Gregory F., and Ronald L. Mullis (1988). "Family Influences on Sexual Attitudes and Knowledge as Reported by College Students." *Adolescence,* Vol. XXIII, No. 92 (Winter), pp. 837–845.

With a total sample of 65 female college students, ages 18–59, single, married and divorced, a self-conducted questionnaire was administered to determine different channels of influence on sex education. The study indicates that parents rate highest (55 percent) in terms of influence; friends rate highest (84.6 percent) in terms of sex information; siblings are the least source of sex information (21.5 percent); and the church was rarely mentioned (10.8 percent). See annotation in Entry 173.

100 Scalrs, Peter, and Mary K. Chelter (1983). *Early Adolescent Sexuality: Resources for Parents, Professionals, and Young People.* North Carolina: Center for Early Adolescence, University of North Carolina at Chapel Hill, 32pp. (ED 238-584).

This publication lists materials recommended for use by parents, professionals and adolescents in sexuality education.

101 Schwartz, Meg, ed., with foreword by Robert Coles (1982). *TV & Teens: Experts Look at the Issues.* Reeling, Mass.: Addison-Wesley, 222pp.

Members of a research group interviewed children between the ages of 8 and 14 to determine why they watched television. The findings published in this volume by social science experts (Comstock, Atkin, Morgan and Gerbner, Sprafkin and Silverman, and Hamburg), and the prose by those who create and produce television programs (Norton Wright, Squire Rushnell, Norman Lear), document the uses and purposes of television for a typical teenager. Particularly, Section 5 on "Sex and Sexuality," provides insight to how the sexually active person is presented on television. Additionally, programs which explore adolescent sexuality, and health issues are discussed. See annotation in Entry 219.

102   Schyller, Ingela, et al. (1986). *Children and Mass Media in Sweden*. Stockholm: Swedish Broadcasting Corporation (February), 34pp.

This analysis focuses on television and the world of children and adolescents in Sweden. It also includes information on sex differences in viewing and why they watch television. Their fear of violence and their norms and values are part of the discussion.

103   Seiter, Ellen (1983). "Men, Sex, and Money in Recent Family Melodrama," *Journal of University of Film and Video Association,* 35(1), pp. 17–27.

The sex curricula on television is prevalent in both daytime and prime-time serials, the author argues here. The study also indicates that sexuality was not only directed to married people, but children.

104   Shapiro, C.H. (1980). "Sexual Learning: The Short-Changed Adolescent Male." *Journal of the National Associates of Social Workers,* Vol. 25, No. 6.

This article examines numerous studies and concludes that the adolescent male does not receive the sexual information that is necessary to prepare him for puberty. One study revealed that in Cleveland, Ohio, between 85 and 95 percent of over 1,400 parents interviewed stated that they never mentioned anything about erotic behavior (intercourse or premarital sex) or its social consequences (pregnancy, venereal disease, abortion) to their children. The same study revealed that less than 2 percent of the fathers and 9 percent of the mothers ever discussed premarital sex with their sons. Another study of 127 parents revealed that 53 percent of the mothers believed that their sons were prepared for nocturnal emissions, but only 9 percent of the fathers stated that they had prepared their son, thus revealing a large discrepancy in what the mothers think and what the fathers do. This study suggests that the home is the best place for an adolescent to learn about sex. Also, the author concludes that it is necessary for the fathers to attend parent meetings to make sure that they are educated enough to explain sex to their adolescent males.

105   Singer, Dorothy G., and Jerome L. Singer (1987). "Television and the Popular Media in the World of the Early Adolescent," *Journal of Early Adolescence* (Special Issue, Fall).

This special issue contains a series of articles which examine the impact of television and the popular media on the early stages of adolescence.

106   Smothers, J. (1961). "The Public and Private Meanings and Uses of Popular Music for American Adolescents." (Ph.D. Dissertation, University of Chicago).

The author concludes that music is an essential ingredient to the romantic rites of dances, parties, and dating so intrinsic to this transitional period of development. In essence, it contributes to the adolescent's learning and how adolescents compose sexual identities.

107   Strasburger, Victor C. (1985). "Television and Adolescents." *Pediatric Annals,* 14(2):814–820.

This study analyzes television within a "chicken-

and-egg dilemma." In other words, it poses the question, Does television reflect society or is television responsible for societal changes relative to sexuality? More specifically, the author addresses the question, Why has the rise in teenage sexual activity coincided with the video explosion of the past 30 years? He argues that teenagers on television are frequently portrayed "in crisis" (drug- or sex-related). Television occasionally discusses premarital sex, or sex education. Thus, television is rife with sexual suggestiveness especially in soap operas—usually popular among teens and preteens. The author suggests, therefore, that every television set ought to have the following label posted on it: "Caution: Too Much or Inappropriate Viewing May Be Hazardous to Your Health."

108 Streenland, Sally (1989). "TV Still Struggling with Teenage Reality," *Media & Values* (Spring) 46:19.
See annotation in Entry 38.

109 "Talking with TV: A Guide for Grown-ups and Kids" (1989). Washington, D.C.: Center for Population Options, 13pp.

This booklet shows numerous ways television can be used by adults to initiate conversations about sex with teens and preteens.

110 Thornburg, Hershel D. (1981). "The Amount of Sex Information Learning Obtained During Early Adolescence." *Journal of Early Adolescence,* Vol. 1, No. 2, pp. 171–183.

This study suggests that there is a disparity between human sexuality and sexual behavior, especially in sexual maturation during early adolescence. This disparity serves as a motivational force in sexual information and learning within the adolescent population. The study reports findings from a survey that was designed to determine the sources of adolescents' first sexual information; sex differences in initial sex information sources; ages at which sexual concepts were first learned; initial sources of sex information by grade; and degree of accuracy of initial sex information. While the reports indicate that 99 percent of initial sex information is learned during early adolescence, females tend to learn from more reliable sources than males.

111 Thornburg, Hershel D. (1972). "A Comparative Study of Sex Information Sources." *The Journal of School Health,* Vol. XLII, No. 2, February, pp. 88–91.

This study indicates that 39 percent of sex information is received from peers. This supports previous studies which found that 37.9 percent of 191 female college students in Arizona and 190 female college students in Oklahoma surveyed received their first source of sex information from their peers.

112 Truglio, Rosemarie (1990). "The Socializing Effects of Prime-Time Television on Adolescents' Learning About Sexuality." (Paper presented at the Center for Population Options Conference, "Teens, TV and Sex," in Los Angeles, July 7–8).

This study investigates how viewing prime-time television programs is related to adolescents' knowledge, attitudes and beliefs about sexuality. Based on the analysis of the data obtained from participants in the study, the author argues that "A direct effect of prime-time television viewing was that girls who were heavy viewers perceived a greater similarity between television couples' contraception use and real life sexual relationships. Indirect effects were also noted."

113   Van Hoose, John H. (1980). "The Impact of Television Usage on Emerging Adolescents." *High School Journal,* Vol. 63, No. 6 (March), pp. 239–243.

> This study indicates the role of media in early adolescence (ages 10–15). It identifies some of the characteristics which directly relate to adolescent exposure to media messages.

114   Wartella, Ellen, and Byron Reeves (1985). "Historical Trends in Research on Children and the Media: 1900–1960." *Journal of Communication,* Vol. 35:2, Spring, pp. 118–133.

> This study analyzes the reflections of scholars on the effects of media on children from 1900 to 1960. The analyses indicate specific trends in research activities of the past six decades.

115   "What You Don't Know About Teen Sex: How Often They Do It, How Little They Tell" (1987). *People Weekly,* April 13.

> The entire issue tackles the issue of teen sexuality. Basically, television is identified as the predominant villain. The argument centers on the following question: "How could teens learn the value of abstinence while watching tails wagging lasciviously in TV commercials for tight jeans?" The cover story indicates that "there were 20,000 instances of 'suggested sexual intercourse' in 1986's TV programming." Other articles and a "Doonesbury" cartoon reflect the theme of this issue.

116   "What's on Tonight? TV Shows with Pre-Teen Appeal" (1989). In *Talking with TV: A Guide for Grown-ups and Kids.* Washington, D.C.: Center for Population Options, pp. 7–12.

> This article describes 17 television shows that are popular with preteens. It also provides the reader

with a brief summary of each program, their air time, and the address of companies that produce each program.

117   White, Barbie (1989). "'Sassy' & 'Seventeen': Do Teen Magazines Reflect or Influence Sexual Attitudes?" *Media & Values,* 46:11.

See annotation in Entry 189.

118   Winship, Elizabeth (1989). "What Teens Ask About Sex." In *Talking with TV: A Guide for Grown-Ups and Kids.* Washington, D.C.: Center for Population Options, p. 1.

The author is a nationally syndicated writer whose advice column for teens, "Ask Beth," is published by over 90 newspapers nationwide. In this article, she argues that when it comes to sex, teens want to know everything.

119   Workman, Diana (1989). "What You See Is What You Think," *Media & Values,* (Spring) 46:2–5.

In the author's analysis of the sexual content of prime-time television, she identifies five problems with television sex. The argument here is that television's most profound lesson is its reflection of the continuing sexual discomfort of the American society.

4 ADOLESCENTS' ATTITUDES AND VALUES

120 "Adolescent Sexuality and the Media" (1987). *The Facts* (January). Washington, D.C.: Center for Population Options.
The fact sheet addresses the role of television and radio; the scope of sex on television; the influence of sexuality-related information on broadcast media; and effects of television on adolescent behavior. While none of the studies cited here establishes a direct relationship between teen sexual behavior and media's sexual messages, taken together they reveal media's potential as positive and negative influence on teen's knowledge, attitudes, values and behavior about sexuality. Includes references.

121 Baran, Stanley J. (1976). "How TV and Film Portrayals Affect Sexual Satisfaction in College Students." *Journalism Quarterly,* Vol. 53, No. 3 (Autumn), pp. 468–473.
This study examines the relationship between television and film portrayals of sexual behavior, and subsequent sexual satisfaction or dissatisfaction in college students who range from 17 to 26. The key findings are as follows: "There are important relationships between the individual's perception of

media portrayals of sex and his or her sexual satisfaction; those who perceived media portrayal of sex as real reported greater satisfaction in their first and subsequent coital experiences; those who saw movie portrayals of sex as being real and those who saw media characters as experiencing greater sexual satisfaction reported less satisfaction in their own state of virginity." Based on these findings, it could be argued that media is a contributing factor to an individual's perception of his or her sexual self.

122   Baran, Stanley J. (1976). "Sex on TV and Adolescent Self-Image." *Journal of Broadcasting,* 20:61–68.

Using a sample of high school students, the author offers evidence that perceptions of the reality after exposure to television portrayal of sexual behavior do affect the level of satisfaction in the initial coital experience of an individual. The students who reported that they saw television portrayals of sexual behavior as accurate also indicated that they were dissatisfied with their first experience with coitus. By the same token, those subjects who saw television characters as their sexual superiors in performance and enjoyment also reported initial coital dissatisfaction. Baran argues that these adolescents generally had little real-life experience against which to judge the televised portrayals and therefore were in no position to perceive them as inaccurate. If they accepted the presentation as real, dissatisfaction would be the likely reaction, the author concludes.

123   Blanchard-Fields, Fredda, Robert Coon, and Robert Mathews (1986). "Inferencing and Television." *Journal of Youth and Adolescence,* Vol. 15, No. 6, pp. 453–459.

In this study, a sampling of 160 youths: 80

adolescents (M = 14 years, 2 months) and 80 young adults (M = 21 years, 9 months) were used. Three-minute segments from each of four prime-time dramas and four music videos served as audiovisual narratives for the experiment. Segments were randomly combined to create four stimulus conditions, consisting of one prime-time drama and one video music segment. The authors concluded that the young adults responded with more elaborative inferences than adolescents; the responses for both age groups were differentially affected by type of television segment; and the more ambiguously structured television segment (i.e. video music) elicited more elaborative inferences for older but not for younger participants.

124   Bloomfield, Kim A., and Diana L. Werkman (1987). "Sexual Behavior on Television: A Content Analysis of the Top Ten Nielsen Rated Programs." Unpublished Study Conducted Through Support by the Center for Population Options in Conjunction with the Nancy Susan Reynolds Award for Sexual Responsibility in the Media. (September).

Using the Top Ten Nielsen rated programs for the fall 1986 season ("Family Ties," "Cheers," "The Cosby Show," "Golden Girls," "Who's the Boss," "Night Court," "Growing Pains," "Dallas," "Moonlighting," and "Murder, She Wrote"), the authors coded and analyzed the sexual contents of three episodes each comprising 19.5 hours of programming. The study documents 10 categories of behavior related to sex. The most prominent are: "touching behavior" (24.5 acts per hour); "suggestion and innuendo" (16.5 times per hour); "sexual intercourse" suggested (2.5 times per hour); and "discouraged sexual practices" (6.2 times per hour).

125   Brown, Marvin, Donald M. Amoroso, and Edward Ware (1976). "Behavioral Effects of Viewing Pornography." *The Journal of Social Psychology,* Vol. 98, pp. 235–245.

Fifty-eight male university students viewed 15 color slides of an attractive couple engaged in a variety of heterosexual activities and masturbation. Of this number, 51 percent of them gave positive emotional reactions while 49 percent expressed negative reactions (guilt, anger, and frustration). There is a general lack of relation between personality and demographic variables and the effects of pornography. Everyone felt sexually aroused, even though they expressed negative emotional reactions. Many reported to have used their imaginations to add to the slides and, presumably, to increase their own sexual arousal. This finding provides some support for theoretical arguments that imagination of sexual activities could be considerably more vivid than those activities explicitly depicted.

126   Cantor, Muriel G., and Joel M. Cantor (1989). "Do Soaps Teach Sex?" *Media & Values,* 46:5.

See annotation in Entry 50.

127   Chamberlin, Leslie J., and Norman Chambers (1979). "How Television Is Changing Our Children." *Clearing House,* Vol. 50, No. 2, pp. 53–57 (October).

The article examines the effects of television on children. It focuses on how television reinforces their overall knowledge, school audience, social attitudes, self image, socialization, desensitization to violence, and increased aggression.

128   Childers, Kim Walsh (1990). "Adolescents' Interpretation of Male-Female Relationships in a Soap Opera." (Paper presented at the Center for Population Options Conference, "Teen, TV and Sex," in Los Angeles, Calif. on July 7–8).

The author examined the effects of gender, sexual experience, sexual schema, television use and the inclusion of explicit discussions of contraception on adolescents; perception of a television portrayal of male-female relationships in a soap opera. The results of the study indicate that adolescents belief in, perceptions about, and intentions to use birth control depends on the version of soap opera and one's own belief. Other perceptions were indicated in the author's report.

129   Childers, Kim Walsh, and Jane Brown (1989). "No Blank Slate: Teen Media Awareness Mirrors Upbringing," *Media & Values,* 46:8–10.

See annotation in Entry 51.

130   Code Research (1981). *Human Sexuality Study, Market Opinion Research for the National Association of Broadcasters,* Washington, D.C.

A majority of the adolescents surveyed for this study indicated that television is equally or more encouraging about sex than either their best male or female friends. Additionally, the respondents believe that public service announcements could serve as appropriate sources of information about sex and birth control.

131   Comstock, G. (1975). "The Effects of Television on Children and Adolescents: The Evidence So Far." *Journal of Communications,* pp. 25–34 (Autumn).

This study summarizes the research findings on the effect of television on children and adolescents. The overall findings show that children develop definite tastes in television programs as early as age three, and tastes are related to age, sex and race; young persons frequently describe television drama as accurately portraying reality, and such a perception is more frequent among those who are black or from families of low socioeconomic status; young persons, like adults, typically believe television news is credible; television affects young persons' attitudes and information, especially on topics where the environment does not supply firsthand experience or other sources of information; the trend of evidence contradicts earlier findings which suggested that television reduces aggression among young people by inducing catharsis.

132   Cullari, Salvatore, and Robert Mikus (1990). "Correlates of Adolescent Sexual Behavior," *Psychological Reports,* 66, pp. 1179–1184.

A sample of 116 Catholic and 92 public high school students was used by the authors to determine the adolescents' sexual knowledge and information about sexual activity. The analysis of data indicate that "33% of the Catholic and 73% of the public 12th graders had previous sexual experience." These findings also identify the factors that encourage sexual experimentation.

133   "D.C. Teenager and AIDS: Knowledge, Attitudes, and Behavior" (1988). Washington, D.C.: Center for Population Options (April), 8pp.

See annotation in Entry 195.

134   Eisen, Marvin, and Gail L. Zellman (1984). "Health Belief Model-Based Changes in Sexual Knowledge, Attitudes and Behavior." (Paper presented as part of the symposium A

Health Belief Model Approach to Improving Adolescent Fertility Control at the Annual Convention of the American Psychological Association 92nd, Toronto, Ontario, Canada, August 24–28), 23pp. (ED 263-499).

A Health Belief Model (HBM)–based educational intervention intended to increase adolescents' fertility control through abstinence or effective contraceptive usage was implemented and evaluated by preintervention interviews with 203 adolescents and postintervention interviews with 146 adolescents. From the HBM perspective, the findings demonstrate substantial relationships between some health beliefs, sexual knowledge, and subsequent contraceptive usage for those adolescents who were or became sexually active following the program.

135   Fernandez-Collado, C.F., B.S. Greenberg, et al. (1978). "Sexual Intimacy and Drug Use in TV." *Journal of Communication,* 28 (Summer), pp. 30–37.

The authors of this study used one episode of each 1976–77 prime-time and Saturday morning dramatic television series to analyze the sexual and drug-related contents in the programs. Three hundred fourth-, fifth-, and eighth-grade school children were surveyed to determine their viewing habits as they relate to the programs under analysis. The result shows that intercourse between unmarried partners was again most frequent at a rate of .60 per hour. The authors concluded that the message sent to viewers is that "[intercourse] occurs quite often, but seldom among those who are married to each other. Further, it can be bought and paid for if not obtained otherwise."

136   Finkel, Madelon L., and David J. Finkel (1975). "Sexual and Contraceptive Knowledge, Attitudes and Behavior of Male

Adolescents." *Family Planning Perspectives,* 7(6), pp. 256–260.

This study is composed of 421 male students from three high schools in a large northeastern city. The analysis of the data collected shows that the initial sexual activity for males begin at 12.8 years of age, although the activity remains sporadic in nature. Ninety-two percent of the respondents said that they use a condom always or many times. At last coitus though, only 28 percent reported using a condom. Of those respondents whose female partners used contraception, 63 percent stated that they never or seldom used a condom. The study also indicates that 30 percent of the males used withdrawal or their partners relied on douche as a means of contraception at last coitus.

137   Fisher, Terri D. (1988). "Characteristics of Parents Who Talk to Their Adolescent Children about Sexuality." (Paper presented at the Annual Meeting of the Society for the Scientific Study of Sex, 31st, San Francisco, California, November 10–13), 9pp. (ED 303-710).

This study identifies variables related to family discussions of sexuality in 290 college students and their parents. It also shows that openness in general family communication and previous sexual discussions with one's mother were related to communication, by both parents, about sex with one's own child. However, educational level and general sexual attitudes were related to sexual communication in the case of fathers only.

138   Fisher, Terri D. (1986). "An Exploratory Study of Parent-Child Communication About Sex and the Sexual At-

Management Internship Registration

NAME: _____

PHONE: _____

BEST TIME TO CALL: _____

WHERE WILL YOU BE LIVING THIS SUMMER? _____

ARE YOU ABLE TO WORK FULL TIME THIS SUMMER?

O YES   O NO

DO YOU HAVE A VEHICLE?   O YES   O NO

WHAT CLASS DID WE SPEAK IN? _____

titudes of Early, Middle, and Late Adolescents," *The Journal of Genetic Psychology* (December), Vol. 147, pp. 543–557.

This study examines the relationship between parent-child communication about sex and parent-adolescent attitudes about sex. Using a sample of 12- to 20-year-olds and their parents, the author found that correlations between parents' and children's attitude were high for early adolescents and low for middle adolescents. This study also suggests that "more responsible sexuality is seen in adolescents who talk to their parents about sex."

139   Fisher, Terri D. (1989). "An Extension of the Findings of Moore, Peterson, and Furstenberg (1986) Regarding Family Sexual Communication and Adolescent Sexual Behavior," *Journal of Marriage and the Family* (August), Vol. 51, pp. 637–639.

Using the findings by Moore, Peterson, and Furstenberg published in the November 1986 issue of the *Journal of Marriage and the Family,* the author examines the relationship between family communication about sexuality and adolescent sexual behavior, attitudes, knowledge, and contraceptive use. The author found that "the relationship between the variables under study differs as a function of gender and parental sexual attitudes as well as the source of the information."

140   Fisher, Terri D. (1988). "Parental Sexual Attitudes, Family Sexual Communication, and Adolescent Sexual Behavior." Paper presented at the Annual Meeting of the American Psychological Association (96th, Atlanta, Georgia, August 12–16), 12pp. (ED 303-711).

Using the variables of gender and parental sexual attitudes (liberal or conservative), the author examined the relationship between family communication about sexuality and adolescent sexual behavior, attitudes, knowledge, and contraceptive use. The author found that a significant positive correlation exists between family sexual communication and conservative sexual attitudes for males with conservative parents. Daughters of liberal and conservative parents were more likely to be sexually active if they had talked to their parents about sex.

141 "43% of Teens in Conservative Churches Have Sexual Relations by 18, Poll Finds" (1988). *Los Angeles Times,* February 6, Section II, Column 1, p. 7.

"Teen Sex Survey in the Evangelical Church" finds that 43 percent of surveyed church-going teenagers engage in sex by age 18. The article is compared with the findings in a Louis Harris and Associates poll in December, 1986, which found that "57% of the nation's 17-year-olds are sexually experienced while 46% of the 16-year-olds and 29% of the 15-year-olds said they had had sexual intercourse."

142 Fouhy, Beth, and Cynthia Thompson (1988). "Media Images: How the Networks Are Handling Teen Sexuality," *CLINIC News* (Support Center for School-Base Clinics, Houston, Texas), Vol. III, No. 4 (January), p. 3.

The authors report on five Kansas City teens' perceptions of how television handles teen sexual behavior and the effect on teen viewers.

143 Franzblau, Susan, Joyce N. Sprafkin, and Eli A. Rubinstein (1977). "Sex on TV: A Content Analysis." *Journal of Communication,* pp. 164–170.

A content analysis of 61 programs, representing the prime-time (Family Viewing Time, or FVT) network programming, was undertaken for one week from all three major networks beginning October 11, 1975. Movies and specials were excluded. Thirteen categories of physical intimacy, ranging from intimate behaviors (e.g., intercourse) to casual behaviors (e.g., embracing), and verbalizations (e.g., innuendo), were coded. The findings indicate that there are "more behavioral acts of non-aggressive touching during FVT (84.9 per hour) than during post–FVT (56.85 per hour). There were more innuendos (with or without canned laughter) appearing during FVT (1.12 per hour) than during post–FVT (.38 per hour). There were also more physically intimate overt behaviors (combined across categories) during FVT (97.2 per hour) than during post–FVT (69.41 per hour)."

144   Fuchs, Lucy (1984). "The Hidden Messages in Children's Books." Paper presented at the Annual Meeting of the Florida Reading Association (22nd, Jacksonville, Florida, October 18–21), 12pp. (ED 252-856).

This paper suggests that you are what you read. It is an analysis of children's books and their portrayal of issues such as drugs and alcohol, sex, birth control, and divorce. The books analyzed here treat most types of sexual behavior as appropriate while emphasizing the problems associated with sexual behavior, its situations, and the need for maturity to deal with it.

145   Greenberg, B.S., D. Graef, C. Fernandex-Collado, et al. (1980). "Sexual Intimacy on Commercial TV During Prime Time." *Journalism Quarterly,* 57:2, pp. 211–215.

This study analyzes the frequency of intimate sexual behavior during 104.5 hours of prime-time programming from fall 1977 to summer 1978. The findings are compared to a similar study conducted in fall 1976. This study found that the instances of sexual acts decreased from 2.22 per hour in 1976 to 1.35 per hour in 1977, and 1.04 in 1978. Although no explanation is offered for the decrease, which seems to go against the general trend of sex on television, the authors suggest that more studies must be conducted before inferring that the instances of sex on television are on the decline. In the earlier 1976 study, it was found that the plots of several shows may have coincidentally been centered around sexuality, while during the weeks of the present study, the shows that were aired dealt with other issues. For all three samples, references to sexual intercourse between unmarried partners was the most prevalent type of behavior, rating .91 instances per hour in 1976, .52 in 1977, and .42 in 1978. In all three years, the figures outnumbered sex between married couples by a ratio of more than 4:1. Additionally, in both 1977 and 1978, the instances of sex increased dramatically after 9 P.M.

146 Greenberg, B.S., and B. Reeves (1976). "Children and the Perceived Reality of Television." *Journal of Social Issues,* 2:4, pp. 86–97.

This study focuses on the general impact of television on children and adolescents without specific reference to the sexual content of each program analyzed. It argues that since sexual behavior is an inevitable part of television programming, the findings can be applied to understanding how television can alter children's attitudes and behavior. Two hundred and one children were selected from the third to sixth grade classes of a suburban Michigan school district in May 1973. When the children's perception of television was tested, a vast majority of them chose programs originally designed and created for adult viewing. Their choice of program is significant because, if children's perception of reality is molded by television, then there is the likelihood that they could be influenced by messages intended for adults, including those with sexual implications. The study also found that perceived realism of television is highest among the lower IQ groups, younger children (third and fourth graders) and those who were avid television viewers. Overall, the children seem to have been less affected in the area of general reality perception than the reality of specific characters. Therefore, the authors conclude that children's perception of reality is especially susceptible to influence by television in areas where they have no prior experiences.

147   Greenberg, B.S., C. Stanley, M. Siemicki, C. Heeter, A. Sederman, and M. Linsangan (1986). "Sex Content on Soaps, and Prime-Time Television Series Most Watched by Adolescents." Unpublished manuscript, Department of Telecommunications, Michigan State University, East Lansing.

This collaborative work documents the most frequently watched soap serials and prime-time television programs by adolescents.

148   Greenberg, Bradley S., David Graef, Carlos Fernandez-Collado, Felipe Korzenny, and Charles K. Atkin (1980). "Sexual Intimacy on Commercial Television During Prime Time." In Bradley S. Greenberg, *Life on Television: Content Analysis of U.S. TV Drama*. Norwood, N.J.: Ablex Publishing, pp. 129–136.

This study analyzes the sexual intimacy seen during prime-time commercial television. It posits that females make up 58 percent of the "agents" and 50 percent of the "targets" of sexual references for the two weeks of prime-time network programs examined that were aired in 1977 and 1978.

149   Greenberg, Bradley S., Renato Linsangan, Anne Soderman, and Carrie Heeter (1988). "Adolescents and Their Reactions to Television Sex." (Report #5 of Project C.A.S.T. — Children and Sex on Television, Department of Telecommunication Technology at Michigan State University).

This is one of a series of research projects funded by the U.S. Department of Health and Human Services. It profiles the kinds of responses adolescents have to mass media sex. Other reports are: #1 — Children and Sex on TV; #2 — Sex Content in R-rated Films Viewed by Adolescents; #3 — Sex Content of Soaps and Primetime Television Series Most Viewed by Adolescents; and #4 — Adolescents and Their Exposure to Television and Movie Sex.

150   Greenfield, Patricia M., Liza Bruzzant, Kristi Koyamatsu, Wendy Stauloff, Karen Nixon, Mollyann Brodie and David Kingsdale (1987). "What Is Rock Music Doing to the Minds of Our Youth? A First Experimental Look at the Effects of Rock Music, Lyrics and Music Videos." *Journal of Early Adolescence,* Vol. 7, No. 3, pp. 315–329.

This study was designed to determine the cognitive effects of rock music lyrics and music videos on adolescents and young adults. This is a report of three preliminary studies. Study 1 shows that the comprehension of lyrics develop with age. Study 2 indicates that music videos provide less stimulation to imagination, and Study 3 confirms the negative effect of music videos on imagination. The overall conclusion is that a rock song evokes and elicits more feelings when it is part of a music video.

151   Haffner, Debra W., and Marcy Kelly (1987). "Adolescent Sexuality in the Media." *SIECUS Report,* (March-April), pp. 9–12.

The authors analyzed media portrayals of sexuality to determine their impact on adolescent sexual behavior. The analysis draws from television, radio, movies and advertisements to conclude that the suggestive behaviors transmitted through these programs serve as sources of information about sexuality for teenagers. The analysis compares two "number one" songs — Madonna's "Papa Don't Preach," which glorifies teenage childbearing, and Tatiana and Johnny's "Detente," which encourages the young to wait until they are mature to have sexual intercourse. The explicit sexual references in these lyrics, the authors argue, impact on adolescents and their sexual attitudes and behavior.

152   Hajcak, Frank, and Patricia Garwood (1988). "Quick-Fix Sex: Pseudosexuality in Adolescents," *Adolescence,* Vol. XXIII, No. 92, pp. 755–760.

This study shows how adolescents between the ages of 14 and 17 misuse sex. It focuses on how the nonsexual needs in adolescents drive sexual behavior, and produce an artificially high sex drive. When nine subjects with different but similar emotional needs were examined to determine what causes them to turn to a "quick-fix" sexual episode, it was found that adolescents use the quick-fix syndrome for emotional support, to relieve anger, and to feel successful.

153   Hansen, Christine H., and Ronald D. Hansen (1988). "How Rock Music Videos Can Change What Is Seen When Boy Meets Girl: Priming Stereotypical Appraisal of Social Interactions," *Sex Role,* Vol. 19, Nos. 5/6, pp. 287–316.

See annotation in Entry 16.

154   Horn, John (1986). "Experts Say Television Is a Factor in Teen Pregnancy Crisis," *The Orange County Register,* (Television Page), Monday, June 16.
See annotation in Entry 205.

155   Kellan, Jeff (1989). "Decoding MTV: Values, Views and Videos," *Media & Values,* 46:15–16.
The author examines music/rock videos to determine their role in adolescent sexual values. The author also argues that because teens/kids spend an average of two hours a day viewing rock videos, it has become a normal part of many young people's routines.

156   Kelley, Kathryn, and Donna Musialowski (1986). "Repeated Exposure to Sexually Explicit Stimuli: Novelty, Sex and Sexual Attitudes." *Archives of Sexual Behavior,* Vol. 15, No. 6, p. 487.
The sample for this study comprises 28 males and 28 females who viewed a color film showing heterosexual genital intercourse utilizing several positions for 11 minutes at 24 hour intervals in four consecutive weekdays. The film was viewed in groups of three and four persons of the same sex. On the fifth day, they watched a different film: either of a couple engaging in nude petting or one showing a different heterosexual couple having sex. The results indicate that negative effect significantly increases with film repetition. As viewing of sex stimuli was repeated, responses grew more negative in nature. Sexual arousal decreased for both male and female participants. However, when the fifth films were shown, responses went back to normal levels.

157   "Kids and Sex: How to Make TV an Ally" (1989). In *Talking with TV: A Guide for Grown-Ups and Kids.* Washington, D.C.: Center for Population Options, pp. 2–4.

See annotation in Entry 75.

158   "Kids and TV: What the Research Shows" (1989). In *Talking with TV: A Guide for Grown-Ups and Kids.* Washington, D.C.: Center for Population Options, pp. 5–6.

This article is an analysis of the research evidence on television sex and its impact on adolescents' perceptions of sex. Because children and adolescents use media as a source of sexual information, "television does influence children's attitudes toward sex and their perceptions of sexual reality, and there may be some relationship between "sexy" television and sexual behavior.

159   Kirby, Douglas, Philip D. Harvey, David Claussenius, and Marty Novar (1989). "A Direct Mailing to Teenage Males About Condom Use: Its Impact on Knowledge, Attitudes and Sexual Behavior." *Family Planning Perspectives,* (January/February), Vol. 21, No. 1, pp. 12–18.

A letter, information/pamphlet and order coupon for free mail-order condoms were sent to an experimental group of teenage males, 16–17 years of age. An experiment was then designed to measure the impact of the mailing on teenagers' knowledge, attitudes and behavior. The result shows that the experimental group was significantly and more likely to have ordered condoms by mail, presumably as a result of having received the free mail-order condom offer. The study has implications for early intervention, through direct mail techniques.

160   Lake, Sara, ed. (1981). *Television's Impact on Children and Adolescents.* Phoenix, Ariz.: Oryx Press, 102pp.

This is a compilation of research and opinion on commercial television's impact on American youths. An impressive subject index is also included to supplement chapters on television viewing habits of children and adolescents; how children perceive television; the impact of television on children and adolescents; and television as a teaching tool. The articles in the final chapter deal with how to improve the situation. It also mentions some of the mediating roles television can play in the development of children and adolescents.

161   Liebert, Robert M., and Joyce Sprafkin (1988). *The Early Window: Effects of Television on Children and Youth.* New York: Pergamon Press, 306pp.

This book examines the effects of television on children and adolescents. It places emphasis on their attitudes, development and behavior. The text also explores the social, political and economic factors which facilitate or mitigate media effects. In general, it documents current theoretical propositions and research activities which attempt to explain the effects of television exposure on children's attitudes, development, and behavior.

162   Meyer, Manfred, and Ursula Nissen (1979). *Effects and Functions of Televisions: Children and Adolescents; A Bibliography of Selected Research Literature, 1970–78.* (Communication Research and Broadcasting Series, No. 2.) New York: K.G. Saur Publishing, Inc., 172pp.

A total of 914 selected bibliographical entries constitute part of this report by the Surgeon General's Scientific Advisory Committee on Television and Social Behavior. The empirical studies, and research reviews in this report, document the impact of the use of television on children and adolescent's personality development and socialization. It also includes references to French and German publications on this subject.

163   Morgan, Michael (1987). "Television, Sex-Role Attitudes, and Sex-Role Behavior." *Journal of Early Adolescence,* Vol. 7, No. 3, pp. 269–282.

This study measures the amount of television viewing, sex-role attitudes, and sex-role behavior of 287 adolescents. The data analyzed indicate that television viewing is an independent contributor to adolescents' sex-role attitudes over time. However, television is not related to their actual behavior. It is also documented that the relationship between viewing and attitude is mediated by behavior. The study concludes that a reciprocal relationship exists between the amount of viewing and the degree of congruency between sex-role attitudes and behavior.

164   Murray, John P., and Susan Kippax (1978). "Children's Social Behavior in Three Towns with Differing Television Experience." *Journal of Communication* (Winter), Vol. 28, No. 1, pp. 19–29.

This study examines the television viewing patterns and subsequent perceptions of Australian children. The findings focus on the children's lifestyle and leisure behavior following exposure to a specific program.

165   National Institute of Mental Health (1982). "Television and Behavior: Ten Years of Scientific Progress and Implications for the Eighties — Summary Report." National Institute of Mental Health, No. 1, Bethesda, Maryland.

This 1982 report by NIMH suggests that American

teenagers rank their peers, parents and the media as the primary channels of influence on their attitudes and behaviors. This report was compiled from data collected from 600 midwestern teenagers who participated in a study designed to determine the source of their information on family planning. The teenagers cited television more often as their primary source of information on family planning.

166 Newcomer, S., and J.D. Brown (1984). "Influences of Television and Peers on Adolescents' Sexual Behavior." Paper presented at the American Psychological Association Meeting in Toronto, Canada, on August 26.

The authors of this study say their findings suggest that a strong and significant relationship exists between the amount of sexually oriented television programs watched (as a proportion of all television viewed) and the probability of an adolescent's having had intercourse.

167 Ornelas, Kriemhild Conee (1987). "The Depiction of Sexuality in Daytime Television Melodrama." (Ph.D. Dissertation, Bowling Green State University, 255pp.)

With the use of over 30 consecutive broadcasts of three popular soap operas ("Days of Our Lives," "The Young and the Restless," and "General Hospital"), which comprise a sample of 90 viewing hours, the author documents how sexuality is portrayed in soap operas, and the context in which sex related behaviors and verbal references occur.

168 Padgett, Vernon R., Jo Ann Brislin-Slutz, and James A. Neal (1989). "Pornography, Erotica, and Attitudes Toward Women; The Effects of Repeated Exposure," *The Journal of Sex Research,* Vol. 26, No. 4, pp. 479–491.

The authors designed two correlational studies to examine the relationship between pornography and attitudes toward women. With 184 psychology students as subjects, it was found that "hours of viewing pornography was not a reliable prediction of attitudes toward women in either sample."

169   Peterson, Dena L., and Karen S. Pfost (1989). "Influence of Rock Videos on Attitudes of Violence Against Women," *Psychological Reports,* Vol. 64, pp. 319–322.

With a sample of 144 undergraduate men who viewed rock videos, the authors determined that exposure to nonerotic-violent rock videos resulted in significantly higher Adversarial Sexual Beliefs scores and ratings of negative affect.

170   Peterson, J., K.A. Moore, and F.F. Furstenberg (1984). "Television Viewing and Early Initiation of Sexual Intercourse: Is There a Link?" Paper presented at the American Psychological Association Meeting in Toronto, Canada, on August 26.

The data analyzed in a longitudinal survey that was completed in 1981 suggest little correlation between the amount of television watched and subsequent initiation of sexual activity for women, and only a slight correlation for men.

171   Planned Parenthood Federation of America, Inc. (1986). *Teen Sexuality Today: Bibliography of Selected Resources.* New York, N.Y.: 27pp. (ED 296-201).

This document is a bibliography of recent publications, books and journal articles that are related to adolescent sexuality and reproductive health. It comprises 11 books and 102 journals, which are divided into 9 areas: sexuality education, contraceptives, parenthood, communication with parents, reproductive health, sexual behavior, school-based programs, teenage life in general, and male involvement.

172   Reis, Janet and Elicia J. Herz (1989). "An Examination of Young Adolescents' Knowledge of and Attitude Toward Sexuality According to Perceived Contraceptive Responsibility," *Journal of Applied Social Psychology,* Vol. 19, No. 3, pp. 231–250.
See annotation in Entry 218.

173   Sanders, Gregory F., and Ronald L. Mullis (1988). "Family Influences on Sexual Attitudes and Knowledge as Reported by College Students." *Adolescence,* Vol. XXIII, No. 92 (Winter), pp. 837–845.
With a sample of 65 female college students between the age of 18 and 59, the authors administered a questionnaire designed to determine channels of influence on their sexual attitudes and knowledge.
See more detailed annotation in Entry 99.

174   Sigal, Janet, Margaret Gibbs, Bonnie Adams, and Richard Derfler (1988). "The Effect of Romantic and Nonromantic Films on Perceptions of Female Friendly and Seductive Behavior," *Sex Roles,* Vol. 19, Nos. 9/10, pp. 545–554.
Two experiments were conducted by the authors to determine the effects of romantic and nonromantic films on perceptions of female friendly and seductive behavior. With a sample of 57 male and 56 female introductory psychology students, the authors found that "exposure to romantic and nonromantic scenarios in the media may produce contrast effects primarily affecting male interpretation of female nonverbal cues.

175   Signorielli, Nancy (ed.) (1985). *Role Portrayal and Stereotyping on Television: Annotated Bibliography of Studies*

Relating to Women, Minorities, Aging, Sexual Behavior, Health, and Handicaps. Westpoint, Conn.: Greenwood Press.

This is a comprehensive annotated bibliography of general studies on role portrayal, stereotyping, sex roles, and sexual behavior and orientation on television.

176   Silverman, L. Theresa, Joyce N. Sprafkin, and Eli A. Rubinstein (1970). "Physical Contact and Sexual Behavior on Prime-Time TV." *Journal of Communication,* 29(1), pp. 33–43.

This is a content analysis of 64 programs presented in prime time during the fall 1977 season. This study provides information on the kinds of physically intimate and sexual behaviors portrayed on prime-time television. The authors found "contextually implied" sexual intercourse occurred most often in movies/specials. The sexual acts in which the object of arousal or mode of gratification is deemed inappropriate by society occurred twice as often in the later viewing hours (about once per hour) than during the family viewing hour (when portrayals appeared about once every two hours). Black females accounted for most of the verbal references to nonsexual aggression (representing only 4.35 percent of all adult characters, accounting for 24 percent of this category), while black males were involved in most of the aggressive child contact. Additionally, the study documents an increased amount of flirtatious behavior, both verbal and visual, on prime-time television. There is also some evidence of sex-role stereotyping, with females more likely than males to act seductively and males more likely than females to act aggressively.

177   Simon, Rogers (1987). "Casual Sex on TV: Part of the Problem." *Los Angeles Times,* January 4.

This article suggests that attitudes about sex and birth control won't change without changes on television. In support of this argument, the author notes that although sex is open on television today, birth control is still viewed as a deep, dark secret. The basic contention here is that because television is part of the problem, responsible sexuality is impossible if television is not part of the solution.

178   Sipes, Sherri (1987). "Teens, Soaps, and Social Perceptions." (M.A. Thesis, Michigan State University, 209pp).

To enable an analysis of the relationship between daytime soap opera viewing and social perceptions and salience of sex amongst teens, the author interviewed 285 high school juniors in spring of 1983. The data analyzed suggests a significant relationship exists between daytime and evening soap opera viewing and illegitimate pregnancies, deaths at childbirth, marriages resulting from pregnancies, and rape. Additionally, daytime viewing was found to be related to the perceived importance of sex to adults. When examined in concrete terms, "specific contingency analyses of perceived reality, isolation, self-degradation, and other channels of information about sex show varied influence of the relationship between exposure and social reality and the salience of sex."

179   Skorlich, Kerry (1989). "'Degrassi Junior High': Series Grapples with Adolescent Issues," *Media & Values,* 46:10.

The author reviews a PBS production, "Degrassi Junior High." In the episode, "A Big Girl Now," a 14-year-old girl contemplates having sex with her new boyfriend. She encounters some sexual expectations which she is not ready to handle. The series is available for purchase or rental from Direct Cinema, Ltd., P.O. Box 69799, Los Angeles, Calif. 90069, or call (213) 652-8000 for more information. The package for sale includes discussion guides and lessons.

180   Strover, Sharon (1990). "Popular Media and the Teenage Sexual Agenda." (Paper presented at the Center for Population Options Conference, "Teens, TV and Sex," in Los Angeles, Calif., on July 7–8).

This study examines how teenagers react to and interpret certain popular media messages. The author argues that "there are considerable differences in how teens react to and decode music videos compared to movies."

181   "Study Shows Church Kids Are Not Waiting" (1988). *Christianity Today,* Vol. 32 (March), 1988, pp. 54–55.

The results of this survey indicate that 65 percent of the 1,500 church youths surveyed have had some type of sexual contact by the age of 18. Forty-three percent have experienced sexual intercourse by 18. Twenty percent of the youth had participated in some sexual experimentaton by the age of 13. The media rank high as a channel of sexual influence. Fifty-seven percent of those surveyed said they received most of their sexual information from the media.

182   Truglio, Rosemarie (1990). "The Socializing Effects of Prime-Time Television on Adolescents' Learning About Sexuality." (Paper presented at the Center for Population Options Conference, "Teens, TV and Sex," in Los Angeles, Calif., on July 7–8).

See annotation in Entry 112.

183   Udry, Richard J. (1988). "Biological Predispositions and Social Controls in Adolescent Sexual Behavior." *American Sociological Review,* Vol. 53 (October), pp. 709–722.

> With a representative sample of 102 males and 99 females drawn from the eighth, ninth, and tenth grade levels, the author argues that mass media show somewhat incomplete correlation between biological (sexual) needs of adolescents and the sociological restraints placed upon adolescents in society.

184   Van Hoose, John H. (1980). "The Impact of Television Usage on Emerging Adolescents." *High School Journal,* Vol. 63, No. 6, pp. 239–43.

> This study documents the role media plays in early adolescence (ages 10–15). It also amplifies the adolescent characteristics that directly relate to media exposure.

185   Vener, Arthur M., and Cyrus S. Stewart (1974). "Adolescent Sexual Behavior in Middle America Revisited: 1970–1973." *Journal of Marriage and the Family,* 36, pp. 728–735.

> This research replicates a 1972 study that used 4,220 male and female adolescents from three communities in Middle America to determine their sexual behavior. In comparison with the previous study, the findings here suggest no evidence of a major revolution in sexual behavior among the adolescents surveyed. However, they indicate a short term (1970 to 1973) increase at the more involved levels of sexuality among 14- and 15-year-olds. The findings suggest a correlation between increased sexual involvement and the use of illicit drugs, alcohol and cigarettes. At higher levels of sexuality, a double standard does not exist between males and females, as it does at lower

levels. The socioeconomic characteristics of the subjects sampled facilitate the application of the findings at a national level.

186   Vener, Arthur M., and Cyrus S. Stewart (1972). "The Sexual Behavior of Adolescents in Middle America: Generational and American-British Comparisons." *Journal of Marriage and the Family,* 34, pp. 696–705.

A survey of 4,220 male and female adolescents from three communities in Middle America was conducted to determine their sexual behavior as compared to British adolescents. Since World War II, there has been no dramatic increase in sexual activity among adolescents. At lower levels of sexual involvement, males tend to have more incidents of activity, whereas at higher levels, male and female involvement is about equal. Compared with studies of British adolescents, the data indicate that the American youth is more precocious until age 21, than it is the British youth who is involved in higher rates of sexual activity. The study also indicates that younger adolescents are involved in less coitus. However, those who were had more than one or two partners.

187   Violence and Sexual Violence in Film, Television, Cable and Home Video (1985). New York: Report of a Study Committee of the Communication Commission of the National Council of the Churches of Christ in the USA, 28pp.

This report examines the problems of exploitative sex in film, cable TV and television. The discussion also includes analysis of media violence. The conclusions indicate the factors which contribute to personal attitude and action of the media audience. Acknowledging that each medium requires different solutions, lines of actions and recommendations are offered. The report includes an impressive bibliography.

188 Weaver, James B., Jonathan L. Masland, and Dolf Zillman (1984). "Effect of Erotica on Young Men's Aesthetic Perception of Their Female Sexual Partners." *Perception and Motor Skills,* 58, pp. 929–930.

The authors exposed male undergraduates to: (a) nature scenes or (b) beautiful versus (c) unattractive females in sexually enticing situations. They later assessed their girlfriends' sexual appeal and evaluated their satisfaction with their mates. The findings are useful in understanding aesthetic appeal as it relates to adolescent sexual satisfaction.

189 White, Barbie (1989). "'Sassy' and 'Seventeen': Do Teen Magazines Reflect or Influence Sexual Attitudes?" *Media & Values,* 46:11.

This article is the author's impression of "the sexual awareness level of magazines competing for the young audience in today's market place." In reflecting her impressions, the author is confronted with the following questions: Should teen magazines deal with sexual issues? And if they do, what do their young readers learn about them?

190 Winship, Elizabeth (1989). "What Teens Ask About Sex." In *Talking with TV: A Guide for Grown-Ups and Kids.* Washington, D.C.: Center for Population Options, p. 1.

See annotation in Entry 118.

5 CONTRACEPTION, PREGNANCY AND HEALTH ISSUES

191   "The Changing Face of AIDS: Adolescents and HIV Infection" (1989). Washington, D.C.: Center for Population Options (April), 22pp.

> This editorial memorandum by CPO examines the changing face of AIDS as demonstrated by the rate of infection amongst adolescents. A discussion on page 13 examines the role news and entertainment media play in educating teens about the risks of AIDS. This document also includes an extensive bibliography.

192   Childers, Kim Walsh (1990). "Adolescents' Interpretation of Male-Female Relationships in a Soap Opera." (Paper presented at the Center for Population Options Conference, "Teens, TV and Sex," in Los Angeles, Calif., on July 7–8).

> See annotation in Entry 128.

193   Consumer Health Information Program and Services (1986). *Bibliography on Teenage Pregnancy.* Carson, Calif., 6pp. (ED 272-621).

> This is a bibliography of resources and information programs and services available to individuals and organizations concerned with adolescent sexuality and pregnancy.

194 "Contraceptive Product Advertising" (1987). *The Facts.* Washington, D.C.: Center for Population Options (January).

This fact sheet provides an overview on the role of broadcast media in contraceptive product advertising. With evidence from studies on public opinion and a brief historical wrap-up, it discusses some of the reasons why major networks refuse to accept advertising for over-the-counter contraceptive products, even though such ads have been broadcast on independent television and cable stations. It also includes references.

195 "D.C. Teenager and AIDS: Knowledge, Attitudes, and Behavior" (1988). Washington, D.C.: Center for Population Options (April), 8pp.

A focus group formed by CPO to assess adolescents' awareness of and attitudes about AIDS found that teenage students were generally well informed about AIDS and how the HIV virus is transmitted; they did not feel that they were at risk, however, and therefore had not changed their behavior.

196 DiClemente, Ralph J., Jim Zorn, and Lydia Temoshok (1986). "Adolescents and AIDS: A Survey of Knowledge, Attitudes and Beliefs about AIDS in San Francisco." *American Journal of Public Health,* 76(12), pp. 1443–1445.

The sample for this study comprises 1,326 students enrolled in Family Life Education classes at 10 high schools in San Francisco Unified School District. A survey was conducted to identify their knowledge, attitudes and beliefs about AIDS. The results indicate that 92 percent of the students knew that AIDS was a sexually transmitted disease; only 60 percent were aware that using a condom reduced the risk of contracting the disease. Eighty-four percent of the students were aware that AIDS could be transmitted through infected blood via a blood transfusion and 81 percent knew that sharing intravenous drug needles was a source of disease transmission. Only 66 percent were aware that AIDS could not be spread by touching someone's personal belongings and 68 percent knew that casual contact did not spread the disease. These findings have implication on adolescent attitudes, knowledge, and belief of STDs.

197   Dryfoos, Loy A. (1988). *Putting the Boys in the Picture: A Review of Programs to Promote Sexual Responsibility Among Young Males.* New York: Carnegie Corporation of New York, 107pp. (ED 300-729).

The program review focuses on pregnancy prevention and sexual activities among young males. Although it documents the real life experiences of adolescent males, the research also focuses on the determinants of adolescent pregnancy — initiation of sexual activity, use of contraception, attitudes toward pregnancy, and the experience of fatherhood. Male outreach and media programs for sex education are also part of this document.

198   Eisen, Marvin, and Gail L. Zellman (1984). "Health Belief Model-Based Changes in Sexual Knowledge, Attitudes and Behavior." Paper presented as part of the symposium A Health Belief Model Approach to Improving Adolescent Fertility Control at the Annual Convention of the American Psychological Association (92nd, Toronto, Ontario, Canada, August 24–28), 23pp. (ED 263-499).

This analysis is designed to determine the impact of a Health Belief Model (HBM)–based educational intervention intended to increase adolescents' fertility control through abstinence or effective contraceptive usage. The implementation of the program was through preintervention interviews with 203 adolescents and postintervention interviews with 146 adolescents. The findings demonstrate substantial relationships between some health beliefs, sexual knowledge, and subsequent contraceptive usage for those adolescents who were or become sexually active following the program.

199   Finkel, Madelon L., and David J. Finkel (1975). "Sexual and Contraceptive Knowledge, Attitudes and Behavior of Male Adolescents." *Family Planning Perspective,* 7(6), pp. 256–260.

This study is composed of 421 male students from three high schools in a large Northeastern city. An analysis of the data shows that the initial sexual activity for males begin at 12.8 years of age, although the activity remained sporadic in nature. Ninety-two percent of the respondents indicated that they use a condom always or many times. At last coitus though, only 28 percent reported using a condom. Of those respondents whose female partners used contraception, 63 percent stated that they never or seldom used a condom. The data further suggests that 30 percent of the males used withdrawal or their partners relied on douche as a means of contraception at last coitus.

200   Foltz, K. (1985). "TV, Sex and Prevention." *Newsweek,* September 9, p. 76.

This article examines the contraceptive advertisements and information seen on television. The analysis centers on a 30-second ad that offers a toll-free number for contraceptive information which the major networks refused to accept, even though some affiliates, independent and cable stations aired the ad. Because contraceptive advertisers are so mindful of the public's sensitivity, the article says, the ads are particularly bland. For this reason there has been no significant public outcry. The article concludes that independent broadcasters are leading the way in contraceptive advertising, and the networks will eventually follow.

201   Gikonyo, Waithira Lucy (1987). "Family Structure, Salience, and Knowledge of Family Planning Methods Among Urban Kenyans." (Ph.D. Dissertation, The University of Wisconsin–Madison, 212pp.)

The author examines "the relationship between family structure, decision-making, and the use of the mass media and interpersonal channels and knowledge of family planning methods among urban Kenyans." This author's analysis documents the impact of mass media on family planning in Kenya. It indicates a relationship between information disseminated by the media, knowledge, and the improvement of family planning methods in Kenya.

202   Goldfarb, Lori, Meg Gerrard, Frederick X. Gibbens, and Thomas Plante (1988). "Attitudes Toward Sex, Arousal, and the Retention of Contraceptive Information." *Journal of Personality and Social Psychology,* Vol. 55, No. 4, pp. 634–641.

The physiological responses of erotophobic and erotophitic women who viewed presentations about contraceptives were monitored to determine learning and retention of sexually relevant material such as contraceptive information. The results indicate that the erotophotic women knew less contraception information before the presentation and were more aroused by the presentation. The arousal, however, did not interfere with the retention of the material.

The results are further discussed in terms of individual differences in reaction to sexual material and their ability to learn, retain, and use contraceptive information.

203   Goldstein, Cynthia (1985). "The Press and the Beginning of the Birth Control Movement in the United States." (Ph.D. Dissertation, The Pennsylvania State University, 294pp.)

This study analyzes press coverage of the birth control movement at four levels: professional, radical, popular, and government publications. The author concludes that even though press coverage of the movement was sporadic, they managed to carry out a persuasive role in the United States.

204   Haignere, Clara S. (1987). "Planned Parenthood Harris Poll Findings: Teens' Sexuality Knowledge and Beliefs." New York: Planned Parenthood Federation of America, Inc. Paper presented at the Annual Children's Defense Fund National Conference — Washington, D.C., March 11–13, 38pp. (ED 286-086).

This study documents the findings of a national public opinion poll conducted by Louis Harris and Associates for Planned Parenthood Federation of America. One thousand 12- through 17-year-olds were polled to determine their knowledge and beliefs about the problem of teenage pregnancy. Over 50 percent said they had sexual intercourse by their 18th birthday. The sexually active respondents indicated that social pressure, followed by curiosity and sexual gratification, were reasons for being sexually active. The majority said they used contraceptives; 50 percent had no sex education in school; only 35 percent had comprehensive sexuality education. Their sources of information include parents (although many respondents said they never discussed sexuality with their parents). Television, according to this sample, gives realistic views of sexually transmitted diseases, pregnancy, the consequences of sex, and family planning.

205   Horn, John (1986). "Experts Say Television Is a Factor in Teen Pregnancy Crisis." *The Orange County Register,* (Television Page), Monday, June 16.

This article cites experts from both medical and educational fields who argue that "television inundates children with a dangerous celebration of carefree (and inconsequential) sex." These charges, which were countered by broadcast executives, were presented at a conference on "Television and Teen Sexual Behavior" held June 14, 1986. Statistics shared with conferees indicate that "while teenagers spend more than 23 hours a week watching television, their pregnancy rate rockets. . . . Eighty percent of teens feel that pressure from television and peers is primarily responsible for teen-age pregnancy."

206   Jeffries, Georgia (1987). "TV and Teenage Sex: Time to Grow Up." Unpublished manuscript prepared for *EMMY* Magazine.

The author argues that a correlation exists between television's avoidance of contraceptives and teenage sex. Television, the author says, portrays sex as wonderful and one of the rites of passage to adulthood, but avoids any discussion of contraception. The following fact is presented to support the impact of television on adolescent sexuality: the average teenager watches 23.5 hours of television a week. When extrapolated, it means that by the time an 18-year-old graduates from high school, he/she would have spent 15,000 hours in front of a television set and only 11,000 hours in the classroom. Moreover, pregnant teenage girls watch more television before becoming pregnant than nonpregnant girls. Thirty-three percent of the pregnant teenage girls chose as their favorite prime-time characters those who are heavily oriented toward sexual behavior. Additionally, 67 percent of the pregnant girls believe that adult relationships, as portrayed on television, are like real life.

207   Kirby, Douglas, Philip D. Harvey, David Claussenius, and Marty Novar (1989). "A Direct Mailing to Teenage Males About Condom Use: Its Impact on Knowledge, Attitudes and Sexual Behavior." *Family Planning Perspectives,* (February/ January) Vol. 21, No. 1, pp. 12–18.

A letter, informational pamphlet and order coupon for free mail-order condoms were sent to an experimental group of teenage males 16–17 years of age. An experiment was designed to measure the impact of the mailing on their knowledge, attitudes and behavior. The result indicates that the experimental group was significantly more likely to have ordered condoms by mail, presumably as a result of having received the free mail-order condom offer. The study has implications for early intervention through direct mail techniques.

208   Koop, C. Everett (1987). Guest Speech on the Topic of "Television in the Age of AIDS" on September 18 in Los Angeles, Calif.

United States Surgeon General C. Everett Koop, in a speech to over 200 leaders in the entertainment field, said, "For many young people, the entertainment industry is the primary sex educator. Your stories and characters influence their sexual attitudes, values and behavior." To receive one free copy of the entire speech, contact the Publications Department, CPO, 1025 Vermont Ave., S.W., Suite 210, Washington, D.C. 20005 or call (202) 347-5700.

209 Lewter, Dean Worth (1985). "The Media Coverage of AIDS: Responses from the Community Most Affected." (M.A. Thesis, Texas Tech. University, 189pp.)

The author examines the impact of media coverage of AIDS (Acquired Immune Deficiency Syndrome) on gay communities with focus on both homosexual and bisexual men and women. The study also measures and documents respondents' media use; their knowledge of AIDS; their opinions about media coverage of AIDS; and their attitudes concerning AIDS related issues.

210 Louis Harris and Associates, Inc. (1985). *Public Attitudes About Sex Education, Family Planning, and Abortion in the United States.* New York: Planned Parenthood Federation of America, Inc., August/September.

This is one of a series of studies conducted by Louis Harris and Associates for the Planned Parenthood Federation of America. The data analyzed indicate that 68 percent of the adults surveyed believe that television games exaggerate their portrayals of people making love. The majority of these adults, 68 percent suggested that more messages on birth control should be aired to counterbalance the exaggerations of television. This is supported by their contention that television does not deal much with the consequences of sex, pregnancy, family planning, or information about sexually transmitted diseases.

211 Louis Harris and Associates, Inc. (1988). *Sexual Material on American Network Television During the 1987–88*

Season. New York: Planned Parenthood Federation of America, Inc., January 26.

This comprehensive study measures the number and frequency of sexually oriented messages depicted on television during the 1987–88 television season. Through this analysis, changes in the sexual content are tracked over time, and the frequency of commercial advertisements and of public service announcements for contraceptives and birth control are measured. About 129 videotaped television shows (totalling 232 half-hour segments) were analyzed. The major findings are summarized as follows: over 27 instances per hour of sexual behavior were portrayed during this season; no references were made to sex education, sexually transmitted diseases, birth control, or abortion to counterbalance the sexual content on television; afternoon television contains almost 50 percent more sexual content than does evening; references to intercourse occur most frequently on night-time serial dramas. Based on these findings, the study concludes that "over time, the number of more direct sexual references has increased, while the number of less direct types of sexual references has declined." The study also acknowledges the fact that noncommercial or public service announcements for contraception or birth control was aired during the period under analysis.

212 Meyer, Manfred, and Ursula Nissen (1979). *Effects and Functions of Television: Children and Adolescents. A Bibliography of Selected Research Literature 1970–78.* Communication Research and Broadcasting Series, No. 2. New York: K.G. Saur Publishing, Inc., 172pp.

This is a bibliography of studies on the uses of

television and its impact on children and adolescents. This work arose from the research that was part of the Surgeon General's Scientific Advisory Committee on Television and Social Behavior findings.

213   Newcomer, Susan F. (1985). "Does Sexuality Education Make a Difference?" New York: Planned Parenthood Federation of America, Inc., 7pp. (ED 269-673).

The discussions of this report revolve around the pros and cons of sexuality education. The research which indicates effectiveness of sexuality education on college students suggests little relevance to teenage sexuality education. The report, which includes 15 references, shows that sexuality education did not increase the likelihood that teenagers would have sexual intercourse or that their values would change as a result of the program. The overall conclusion drawn here is that sexuality education can be useful in continued and improved access to contraception, and safe legal abortion.

214   Planned Parenthood Federation of America, Inc. (1982). *Sexuality Education Can Make a Difference: Reference Sheet 1 and Bibliography of Selected Resources.* New York: Planned Parenthood Federation of America, Inc. (April), 14pp. (ED 271-644).

This report contains 35 citations, from 1970 to early 1980s. The issues covered here range from teenage pregnancy to contraception.

215   Planned Parenthood Federation of America, Inc. (1986). *Teen Sexuality Today: Bibliography of Selected Researches.* New York: Planned Parenthood, 27pp. (ED 296-201).

This is a selected bibliography of recent publications — books and journal articles — dealing with adolescent sexuality and reproductive health. The 11 books and 102 journals which comprise this document are divided into 9 areas: sexuality education, contraception, parenthood, communication with parents, reproductive health, sexual behavior, school-based program, teenage life in general, and male involvement.

216 "Portraying AIDS in the Media." Century City, Calif.: Entertainment Industry Coalition on AIDS, Center for Population Options (Undated).

This is a guideline for the entertainment industry on portraying AIDS in the media. While it is not intended to limit the creative process, this provides writers and other creative personnel with ideas on how AIDS should be portrayed in the media.

217 Price, James H., Sharon Desmond, and Gary Kukulka (1985). "High School Students' Perceptions and Misperceptions of AIDS." *Journal of School Health,* 55, pp. 107–109.

A survey of 118 males and 132 females, 16–19 years of age, was conducted to determine the level of knowledge, type of beliefs, and sources of information about AIDS among the sample. Overall, the study found that the students had a very limited knowledge of the disease, although males were more knowledgeable than females. It also shows that their primary sources of information about AIDS were television, newspapers, magazines and radio. The majority of students surveyed said they were not concerned about contracting the disease.

218 Reis, Janet, and Elicia J. Herz (1989). "An Examination of Young Adolescents' Knowledge of and Attitude Toward Sexuality According to Perceived Contraceptive Responsibility,"

Journal of Applied Social Psychology, Vol. 19, No. 3, pp. 231–250.

> With a sample of 442 young adolescents from an inner city Chicago public high school, the authors examined knowledge of and attitude toward sexuality according to perceived contraceptive responsibility. The results of the study show contradictions between males' and females' knowledge of and attitudes toward sexuality.

219   Schwartz, Meg (ed.), with foreword by Robert Coles (1982). *TV and Teens: Experts Look at the Issues.* Reading, Mass.: Addison-Wesley, 222pp.

> This book is a compilation of findings from a research group that interviewed children between the ages of 8 and 14 to determine why they watch television. The findings have implications about adolescent sexuality and health issues, such as STDS.
> See more detailed annotation in Entry 101.

220   Simon, Rogers (1987). "Casual Sex on TV: Part of the Problem." *Los Angeles Times,* January 4.

> This article is a discussion on television portrayal of sex and birth control methods. It notes that irresponsible portrayals in the media contribute to sexuality problems in the United States.
> See more detailed annotation in Entry 177.

221   Sipes, Sherri (1987). "Teens, Soaps, and Social Perceptions." (M.A. Thesis, Michigan State University, 209pp).

> This study examines the relationship between daytime soap opera viewing, social perceptions, and salience of sex among teens. To document this, the author interviewed 285 high school juniors in the spring of 1983. The data analyzed suggest that there

is a significant relationship between daytime and evening soap opera viewing and illegitimate pregnancies, deaths at childbirth, marriages resulting from pregnancies, and rape. Additionally, viewing was found to be related to the perceived importance of sex to adults. "Specific contingency analyses of perceived reality, isolation, self-degradation, and other channels of information about sex show varied influence of the relationship between exposure and social reality and the salience of sex."

222 Steinbrook, Robert (1989). "'Surprising' Level of AIDS Reported in Young Teens," *Los Angeles Times,* June 6, Section I, Column 1, pp. 1, 26.

This story reflects findings presented at the Fifth International Conference on AIDS. In this study, the U.S. Center for Disease Control reports that a surprising number of American teenagers are becoming infected with the AIDS virus during early adolescence. The report was part of an ongoing "sentinel" hospital surveillance for AIDS virus infections. The study includes statistical distribution of infection rate at "sentinel" hospitals, blacks and Latinos.

223 Stone, Rebecca, and Cynthia Waszak (1989). "Teenage Pregnancy and Too-Early Childbearing: Public Costs, Personal Consequences." Washington, D.C.: Center for Population Options (September), 18pp.

The authors discuss the problem of teenage pregnancy and its consequences. Included in this discussion is CPO's national priorities list for reducing teen pregnancy and too-early children. One of the 10-point priorities is the role television and other media can play in "advertising of contraceptives prophylactics for the prevention of pregnancy and sexually transmitted disease.

224 "Teen Pregnancy Prevention: You, Run a Media Campaign?" (1988). *Options* (Center for Population Options), Vol. 1, Issue I (Spring), pp. 1, 6.

This article discusses how media campaigns are used to prevent teen pregnancy in some cities. Most campaigners use posters, newspaper ads, subway and bus placards, music videos, rock and rap songs, contests, television and radio public service announcements.

225 Tumulty, Karen (1989). "Schools Held to Avoid Sex Education," *Los Angeles Times,* May 3, Section I, Column 4, p. 16.

According to a report released by the Alan Guttmacher Institute (see Entry 229 for address), as schools focus more of their attention and resources on preventing AIDS, most are not putting enough emphasis on teaching teenagers how to avoid pregnancy, either through abstinence or contraception.

226 United Nations (1988). *Adolescent Reproduction Behavior: An Annotated Bibliography.* New York: United Nations Population Division Report No. — IESA/P/WP/100, 291pp.

This document is a compilation of data housed by universities and population agencies. It contains annotated entries on adolescent and reproduction behaviors. It also includes health aspects of adolescent child bearing and medical risks.

227 United States. Senate. Committee on Labor and Human Resources. Subcommittee on Aging, Family and Human Services (1982). *Health Aspects of Adolescent Sex.* Hearing Before the Senate Subcommittee . . . of the (Ninety-Seventh Congress, Second Session) on Examination of the Alarming Increase in the Rate of Sexual Relations Among Adolescents, 96pp. (ED 233-252).

The discussions during this hearing include findings from the medical profession and family planning experts. This document sheds more light on the alarming increase in the rate of sexual relations among adolescents.

DIRECTORY OF ORGANIZATIONS

Following are selected research institutions and self-help organizations that provide services in the United States. While adolescent issues are not the primary objective of some of these organizations, they do enhance our understanding of some factors that affect the development of adolescents.

The research activities, audiovisual materials, and strategies of these organizations can serve as useful tools for further research on the relationship between mass media portrayals of sex and the construction of sexual reality by adolescents.

The entries identify each research institution and self-help organization, address, telephone number, and fax number when possible. These are followed by a description of their responsibilities and the functions they perform. These entries should not be considered as inclusive of all research institutions or providers of services to adolescents.

Selection of the entries was based on the editor's perception of the importance they play in understanding adolescent development — from their sexuality to media portrayals of sex, from birth control to pregnancy to abortion, and sexually transmitted diseases.

This directory accommodates organizations that disagree on how sex and sexually related issues should be handled or described; for example, groups on both sides of the abortion issue are represented.

228 AIDS International
P.O. Box 2008
Saratoga CA 95070
(408) 866-6303
Fax (408) 866-0825

The AIDS epidemic has given birth to organizations such as this one. Its main objective is to educate the entire population on AIDS sex education. This is accomplished through the periodic publication of titles such as "The A.I.D.S. Catalog" and "Teaching About A.I.D.S.," designed for those who teach at grade levels 5–12 and college. Its sources include books, current bibliographies, and curriculum guides.

229 Alan Guttmacher Institute (AGI)
111 Fifth Avenue
New York NY 10003
(212) 254-5827
Fax (212) 254-9891

The AGI activities emphasize research and public education on family planning and sex education. The Institute publishes a newsletter called *Washington Memo,* which tracks and analyzes legislative actions within its goals. It also publishes a bimonthly *Family Planning Perspectives,* and a quarterly, *International Family Planning Perspectives.*

230 American Alliance Publications
1900 Association Drive
Reston VA 22091
(703) 476-3400
Fax (703) 476-9527

The Alliance consists of eight associates that deal with physical education and health related information. With its international associations, the organization provides research information in a variety of areas. Its publications include a newsletter, *Update,* and a magazine, *The Journal.*

231   American Association of Sex Educators,
        Counselors and Therapists (AASECT)
435 N. Michigan Avenue, Suite 1717
Chicago IL 60611
(312) 644-0828

The AASECT provides continuing education information for professional training for sex educators, therapists, and counselors. It also publishes a monthly newsletter and a quarterly *Journal of Sex Education and Therapy.* They also conduct workshops and an annual conference. Requests for information should be sent in writing.

232   American Citizens Concerned for Life Education Fund
P.O. Box 179
Excelsior MN 55331
(612) 474-0885

Although this nonprofit organization provides valuable materials on abortion, adoption, ethics, sex education and teenage pregnancy, its effort is geared toward the antiabortion movement. A "Resource Catalog," distributed by the organization, contains the literature they publish.

233   American College Health Association
1300 Piccard Drive, Suite 200
Rockville MD 20850
(301) 963-1100
Fax (301) 330-6781

This is a professional nonprofit organization devoted to serving health care professionals on college campuses nationwide. Established since 1920, it represents institutional and individual members. It publishes a variety of materials, including health care brochures.

234   American Educational Films
P.O. Box 8188
Nashville TN 37207
(800) 822-5678

AEF is responsible for numerous films which present adolescent issues in a simplistic way. Its collection includes films which utilize quiz formats to portray adolescents as they encounter their sexuality.

235   American Red Cross AIDS Education Office
1709 New York Avenue, NW
Suite 208
Washington DC 20006
(202) 639-3223
Fax (202) 662-1555

This organization offers a variety of services which relate to AIDS. Check local Red Cross chapters for specific services and questions.

236   American Social Health Association (ASHA)
P.O. Box 13827
Research Triangle Park NC 27709
(919) 361-2742
Fax (202) 548-4048

The ASHA operates national hotlines, develops educational materials and funds research on sexually transmitted diseases. It publishes a quarter journal entitled *The Helper*. The organization's publications include *The Truth About Herpes* and *Questions and Answers About AIDS*.

237   Association of Childhood Education International
       (ACEI)
11141 Georgia Avenue, Suite 200
Wheaton GA 20902
(301) 942-2443

This organization emphasizes comprehensive developmental issues from infancy to early adolescence. With the use of booklets, curriculum guides and newsletters, the organization serves as a network for the distribution of literature on adolescent development and child abuse. The ACEI publications, such as *Early Adolescents: Understanding and Nurturing Their Development,* have been useful for comprehensive involvement in adolescent development. The organization also hosts conferences and organizes workshops.

238   Blackside Films
486 Shawmut Avenue
Boston MA 02118
(617) 536-6900
Fax (619) 536-1732

As a major distributor of films and documentaries, this company has a superb collection of materials which include interviews with teenagers. Its titles include *A Matter of Respect,* which also has excerpts from a speech on sexual responsibility by Jesse Jackson.

239   Cambridge Documentary Films
P.O. Box 385
Cambridge MA 02139
(617) 354-3677

This organization has contributed its share to the development of adolescents. In the process, it has produced films which illustrate the impact of media on perceptions of male and female roles in society.

240   The Center for Disease Control
1600 Clifton Road NE
Atlanta GA 30333
(404) 639-3311
Fax (404) 639-3070

This agency provides national leadership in the prevention and control of diseases. It has published numerous pamphlets on AIDS and other sexually transmitted diseases.

241   The Center for Early Adolescence
The University of North Carolina at Chapel Hill
Suite 223, Carr Mill Hall
Carrboro NC 27510
(919) 966-1148
Fax (919) 966-7657

This center, through its activities, provides professionals, volunteers and policy makers the information and training they need to help adolescents adjust to society. Its services of referrals, site support, policy advocacy, and seminars help those involved in adolescent development to make appropriate decisions. The center's publications include a newsletter, *Common Focus,* and an annotated bibliography of nonfiction publications called *Resources for Young Adolescents.*

242   Center for Population Options (CPO)
National Office
1025 Vermont Avenue, NW
Suite 210
Washington DC 20005

(202) 347-5700
Fax (202) 347-2263

The CPO is a national, nonprofit organization with branches in Houston and Studio City, CA. The CPO serves as a clearinghouse for sex education information that is needed to reduce unintended adolescent pregnancy. The organization's projects include: Partnership Programs—to prevent teen pregnancy and HIV infection; Life Planning Education; Public Policy; School-Based Clinics; Media Project; International Clearinghouse on Adolescent Fertility; and a research program to provide program evaluation, information systems technology, and information about teen sexual behavior. The organization facilitates its activities by publishing numerous periodicals intended to help teens "understand that the choices they make regarding sexuality are directly linked to their options in life."

243   Center for Research and Education in Sexuality
San Francisco State University
Psychology Building, Room 502
San Francisco CA 94132
(415) 338-1137

This is an interdisciplinary research and educational unit of the Human Sexuality Studies program at San Francisco State University. It was founded in 1975. It seeks to bridge the humanities and behavioral, social, and biological sciences to human sexuality. Their publications include *Journal of Homosexuality* and a "Research Monograph Series."

244   Center for Research on the Influence
        of Television on Children
University of Kansas
Department of Human Development

Lawrence KS 66045
(913) 864-4646
Fax (913) 864-5323

This center was established in 1977 to document the impact of television on children's cognitive and social behavior. Most of the research evaluates the forms, formats, and production features used to inform and educate children. Its database includes television viewing diaries of more than 326 families and a tape library of most children's programs shown over the past ten years. Most of their research can be seen in journals or book chapters. Some are presented at scientific conferences.

245   Center for the Study of Child
and Adolescent Development
Pennsylvania State University
107 Amy Gardner House
University Park PA 16802
(814) 863-2539

The main function of this center is to promote research in child and adolescent development. Although the results of their studies are published in a "Scholarly Report Series" and a "Technical Report Series," they are accessible and easily comprehensible by those charged with nurturing child and adolescent development.

246   Child Welfare League of America, Inc.
440 First Street, NW
Suite 310
Washington DC 20001
(202) 638-CWLA
Fax (202) 638-4004

To facilitate its services of promoting child welfare, legislative advocacy, conferences, consultancy, and training, the organization uses print and nonprint materials to develop curriculum guides and handbooks. Some of the issues covered include adolescent development, AIDS, parenting, and teenage pregnancy.

247   Children's Defense Fund
122 C Street, NW
Washington DC 20001

This nonprofit organization deals with issues which range from media awareness and legislative advocacy to technical help for children. With publications in English and Spanish, it also serves a clearinghouse for prevention of adolescent pregnancy.

248   Concerned Women of America
370 L'Enfant Promenade
Suite 800
Washington DC 20024
(202) 488-7000
Fax (202) 488-0806

The focus of this group is adolescent pregnancy and health. Its publications include *Teen Pregnancy* and *School-Based Health Clinic*.

249   Counseling and Personnel Services Clearinghouse
2108 School of Education
The University of Michigan
Ann Arbor MI 48109-1259
(313) 764-9492

The CPSC is part of the ERIC organization. Its main focus is to collect data and educational materials on counseling and personnel services. This includes research on adolescent development, AIDS, family, marriage, and teenage pregnancy. The summary of these studies can be found in the ERIC database.

250   Documents Associates
The Cinema Guild
1697 Broadway, Suite 802
New York NY 10019
(212) 246-5522

This organization distributes films and audiovisual materials, some of which deal with adolescent sexuality and sexual experiences. Its list of productions includes *All the Guys Ever Want Is Sex,* a discussion of adolescent sexuality.

251   Education, Training and Research Associates (ETR)
4 Carbonero Ways
Scotts Valley CA 95066
(408) 438-4284
Fax (408) 438-4284

The organization devotes its efforts to teaching family life education. It publishes a quarterly magazine, *Family Life Education.*

252   Encyclopaedia Britannica Educational Corp.
425 N. Michigan Avenue
Chicago IL 60611
(312) 321-8000

With a wealth of resources, this corporation is contributing to awareness of issues which affect adolescents and other groups. One of the outstanding strategies used by this organization is the design of information campaign programs for the hard-to-reach adolescent population. Its interactive computer program, "Body Awareness Resources Network" (BARN), is an information campaign program which can be run on any Apple II computer with 64K memory.

253   Entertainment Industry Coalition on AIDS
Center for Population Options
12023½ Ventura Blvd., Suite 2
Studio City CA 91604
(818) 766-4200
Fax (818) 766-3561

>   Formed by the Center for Population Options (see Entry 242), this coalition is composed of the three big television networks, independent stations, production companies, and representatives of directors, producers, publicists, writers, and actors. The publication *Portraying AIDS in the Media* is one of the organization's resources. Designed to suggest how the entertainment industry can portray AIDS in the media, it is not intended to limit the creative process.

254   Family Life Information Exchange
P.O. Box 10716
Rockville MD 20850
(301) 770-3662

>   This organization's database and publications provide information on adolescent pregnancy, family planning, abortion, and sex education. One of its publications is entitled *Adolescent Family Life Research Projects Summary: Adolescent Sexual Behavior/Adoption.*

255   Film and Television Documentation Center
State University of New York at Albany
Rich 390C
1400 Washington Avenue
Albany NY 12222
(518) 442-5745

>   This center serves as a clearinghouse for scholars interested in the subject of film and television docu-

mentation. Founded in 1981, it also publishes a comprehensive bibliographic quarterly, *Film Literature Index*. Additionally, it provides access to film and television journals and articles related to this field.

256   Films Inc.
5547 N. Ravenswood
Chicago IL 60640
(312) 878-2600 ext. 43
(800) 323-4222 ext. 43

This organization uses noted personalities, such as Bryant Gumbel (NBC), to reach high-risk adolescents. One of its productions, *Main Street: Sex and the American Teenager,* reveals some attitudes adolescents have about sexuality.

257   Ford Foundation
320 East 43 Street
New York NY 10017
(212) 573-5169

This is a private, nonprofit philanthropic organization among whose interests are adolescent development and birth control. *Ford Foundation Publications and Films* lists all materials published and distributed by the organization.

258   Gay Men's Health Crisis
Box 274
132 West 24th Street
New York NY 10011
(212) 807-6655
Fax (212) 337-3656

This organization, which was formed in 1981, is the oldest and largest AIDS organization in the nation. It provides services, education, and advocacy for people infected with HIV virus. Currently, it serves 3,000 people with AIDS. Additionally, it educates the public and advocates for fair and effective AIDS policies at the city, state, and federal level. It has a number of publications and brochures. It also publishes a newsletter called *Volunteer*.

259   Guidance Associates
Communications Park
Box 3000
Mount Kisco NY 10549-9989
(800) 431-2266

The distribution list of this organization includes filmstrips, and audio and video tapes on a variety of subjects. The adolescence and sexuality component has titles such as *Adolescence: Changing Values* and *Who You Are and What You Are: Understanding Sex Roles*.

260   Kaw Valley Films & Video, Inc.
P.O. Box 3900
Shawnee KS 66203
(913) 631-3040

This corporation markets programs which emphasize adolescent development. Some of these programs use dramatic experiences by teenagers to explore the options available to those who are faced with sexual intimacy decisions.

261   The Kids on the Block, Inc.
9385-C Gerwig Lane
Columbia MD 21044
(800) 368-KIDS (5437)
Fax (301) 290-9358

This worldwide organization is in its fourteenth

year of operation. It has puppet programs in 50 states and 23 countries. Large size puppets are used to teach children to accept and appreciate persons with disabilities, medical differences, and social concerns. Puppet characters represent children who are blind, deaf, mentally retarded, and learning disabled. Puppet programs are used for the prevention of drug and alcohol abuse, teenage pregnancy and AIDS, and other topics. Volunteers operate the puppets. The puppet program received the Surgeon General's Medallion for Excellence in Public Health in 1989.

262   Kinsey Institute for Research in Sex, Gender, and Reproduction
313 Morrison Hall
Indiana University
Bloomington IN 47405
(812) 335-7686

The institute is a nonprofit research organization affiliated with Indiana University. Its collections include archives of materials on sex, gender, and reproduction research. They disseminate research information through publications such as *Annotated List of AudioVisual Materials with Sexual Content.* In addition to its publications, the institute maintains a statistical database on human sexual behavior. Their services include an information service that responds to telephone or written requests; they provide bibliographies based on the Institute's unique collections, and perform data runs.

263   Laboratory for the Study of Adolescence
Michael Reese Hospital
2959 South Cottage Grove Avenue
Chicago IL 60616
(312) 791-3865

This research organization conducts studies on different areas of adolescent development. It was established in 1968. Some of its research activities include factors related to sex differences in cognition. This lab has also accumulated findings on young adult and adolescent decision-making about contraception; the relationship between sex role identity in adolescence and the performance of spatial tasks; and the self-image of adolescents in different cultures. They offer training programs, weekly research seminars, and sponsor an annual conference on adolescence in June.

264   Learning Corporation of America
1350 Avenue of the Americas
New York NY 10019
(212) 397-9360

The LCA has played a prominent role in the struggle to increase awareness among adolescents. Some of their efforts are captured in films and documentaries which are widely distributed out of their New York City office.

265   McGraw-Hill Films
110 15th Street
Del Mar CA 92014
(714) 453-5000

This film division of McGraw-Hill is an important source for materials on adolescent sexuality. In some of their films, young people are encouraged to develop their personalities free from sex role stereotypes, and to aim at self-actualization.

266   Media Action Research Center (MARC)
1962 S. Shenandoah

Los Angeles CA 90034
(213) 559-2944

This is a nonprofit educational organization whose main objective is to research the impact of television on viewers. In the process, it makes available resources about media's influence on society. The organization also publishes its findings and resource materials in its quarterly magazine, *Media & Values*.

267 National Family Planning and Reproductive Health Association, Inc.

122 C Street, NW, Suite 380
Washington DC 20001
(202) 628-3535
Fax (202) 737-2690

The Association acts as a national communication network for the improvement of family planning and reproductive health issues. *NFPRHA News* and *Report* are its basic publications. It has issued position papers on sex education, contraceptive use, adolescent clients, and other topics.

268 National Public Radio

2025 M Street, NW
Washington DC 20036
(800) 253-0808

The NPR is a nonprofit corporation whose programs include discussions of sexual behavior on television. Its cassette division distributes such programs.

269 Network Publications

ETR Associations
P.O. Box 1830
Santa Cruz CA 95061-1830
(408) 438-4080
Fax (408) 438-4284

Network is a division of a nonprofit organization, Education, Training and Research Associates. They distribute hard-to-find materials and also publish materials on family planning, sexuality education, and AIDS. These include works such as *AIDS—Think About It,* also available in Spanish.

270   New Day Films
22 Riverview Drive
Wayne NJ 07470
(201) 633-0212

New Day Films' list of adolescent packages includes *Am I Normal?,* a 22-minute documentary that captures the real life story of a 13-year-old as he discovers that his body is going through certain biological changes.

271   Office of Population Affairs
US Department of Health and Human Services
Room 736-E
200 Independence Avenue, SW
Washington DC 20201
(202) 245-0142
Fax (202) 245-6498

The main function of this government agency is to create and monitor social policies and programs. Its main publication is called *The Family and Adolescent Pregnancy.*

272   Perennial Education, Inc.
930 Pitner Avenue
Evanston IL 60202
(800) 323-9084
Fax (708) 328-6706

This organization is the distributor of educational

films and audiovisuals that also focus on adolescent issues. Among its collection are titles such as *A Family Talks About Sex, AIDS in Your School, Are You Ready for Sex?* and *Teen Sexuality: What's Right for You?*

273   Planned Parenthood Federation of America, Inc.
810 7th Avenue
New York NY 10019
(212) 541-7800
Fax (212) 245-1845

This organization supports family planning and provides contraceptive counseling and services through its 190 affiliated clinics in the United States. The organization publishes numerous works, such as *Guide to Birth Control: Seven Accepted Methods of Contraception; Teensex?; It's OK to Say No Way; A Man's Guide to Sexuality; About Childbirth;* and *Emphasis.*

274   Project Respect
P.O. Box 97
Golf IL 60029-0039
(708) 729-3298

This organization was created by concerned parents to encourage sexual abstinence. It distributes *Sex Respect,* a sex education curriculum.

275   Project SHARE
P.O. Box 2309
Rockville MD 20852
(202) 252-4518
Fax (202) 252-4683

The improvement for human services is the main objective of this organization. In the process, it abstracts related materials and provides bibliographies on adolescent development, AIDS, teenage pregnancy, and other issues. The organization publishes numerous materials, including *Sharing,* a 6-page newsletter.

276   Public Broadcasting Service
Video Division
1320 Braddock Place
Alexandria VA 22314
(703) 739-5380
(800) 424-7963

As a nonprofit organization, PBS emphasizes the publication of educational materials that are useful to its viewers. In this capacity, it has plunged itself into adolescent issues, sexuality and sexually transmitted diseases. Researchers should consider PBS as one of their sources for information on adolescent issues.

277   Pyramid Film & Video
P.O. Box 1048
Santa Monica CA 90406
(213) 828-7577
(800) 532-0118
(800) 421-2304
Fax (213) 453-9083

This organization's collection includes *About AIDS*, a 15-minute video which examines the what and the how of this disease as well as preventive measures.

278   San Francisco AIDS Foundation
333 Valencia Street, 4th Floor
San Francisco CA 94103
(415) 864-4376
Fax (415) 864-5855

This organization provides educational programs, direct service programs, and public policy initiatives. These services are facilitated through the publication of comic books, and teen videos that promote discussion on AIDS.

279   Search Institute
122 W. Franklin Avenue, Suite 525
Minneapolis MN 55404-9990
(612) 870-9511
Fax (612) 870-4602

> The Institute publishes a sex education curriculum, *Human Sexuality, Values and Choices.* Its main function is to promote sexual values through information and social services to adolescents.

280   Sex Education Coalition
P.O. Box 3101
Silver Spring MD 20918
(301) 593-8557

> The SEC is a coalition of health and education professionals, clergy, parents, policymakers, and other concerned citizens in the Washington, D.C., area. They ensure that sexuality education programs present accurate information, provide opportunity for dialogue, and respect differing family and cultural values. The Coalition offers workshops and sponsors meetings for top-level professionals and provides schools, youth groups, and other organizations with technical assistance. Its media catalog and loan services make resources affordable. Its nationally recognized publications include *What Is Sex Ed Really?, Tips for Parents: Talking with Your Children About Sexuality,* and *Media Catalog,* an annotated list of available family life education films and film strips.

281 Sex Information and Education Council
  of the US (SIECUS)
130 West 42nd Street, Suite 2500
New York NY 10036
(212) 819-9770
Fax (212) 819-9776

The SIECUS is a nonprofit health education organization which serves as a clearinghouse for information on sexuality. It compiles bibliographical
resources on human sexuality. In addition to distrib-
uting the videotapes *Just Wait* and *Saving Sex for
Marriage,* the organization publishes the bimonthly
SIECUS Report, and several flyers.

282 Society for the Scientific Study of Sex
P.O. Box 29795
Philadelphia PA 19117

This international, nonprofit research association
was founded in 1957. It supports research on sex. Its
main publications are *Journal of Sex Research* and
Annual Review of Sex Research. It also sponsors annual national and regional meetings and conferences.

283 Sunburst Communications
Room GN2
29 Washington Avenue
Pleasantville NY 10570
(800) 431-1934
Fax (914) 769-9211

The works produced and marketed by this organization are about such issues as sexuality and sexual
responsibility. Some of its films also discuss the possible physical and emotional consequences of adolescents' sexual behavior.

284   US Public Health Service
Public Affairs Office
Herbert H. Humphrey Building
Room 725-H
200 Independence Avenue, SW
Washington DC 20201
(202) 245-6867
Fax (202) 245-6608

> This government agency provides sexuality infor-
> mation through publications such as *AIDS, Sex and
> You, Facts About AIDS and Drug Abuse,* and *AIDS
> and Your Job.*

285   Women's AIDS Project
8235 Santa Monica Blvd., Suite 201
West Hollywood CA 90046
(213) 650-1508

> This organization was established to provide sup-
> port for women with AIDS. It also publishes a
> pamphlet entitled *Women Address AIDS.*

SUGGESTIONS FOR FURTHER READING

Books

Berkowitz, L., and K.H. Rogers (1986). "A Primary Effect Analysis of Media Influences." In J. Bryant and D. Zillman (eds.), *Perspectives on Media Effects*. Hillsdale, N.J.: Erlbaum.

Collins, W.A. (1979). "Children's Comprehension of Television Content" in E. Wartella (ed.), *Children Communicating: Media and Development of Thought, Speech, Understanding*. London: Sage.

Durkin, K. (1985). *Television, Sex Roles and Children*. Philadelphia: Open University Press.

Green, D.L. (1982). *Sex on TV: A Guide for Parents*. Santa Cruz: Network Publication.

Gross, L., and S. Jeffries-Fox (1978). "What Do You Want to Be When You Grow Up, Little Girl?" in G. Tuchman, et al. (eds.), *Hearth and Home: Images of Women in the Mass Media*. New York: Oxford University Press.

Hong, Kisum (1978). *Developmental Aspects of Children's Impression Formations of Television Characters*. University of Minnesota, 216pp.

Further Reading

Liebert, R.M., J.N. Sprafkin, and E.S. Davidson (1982). *The Early Window: Effects of Television on Children and Youth*. New York and Oxford: Pergamon.

Morgan, M., and G. Gerbner (1982). "TV Profession and Adolescent Career Choices" in M. Schwarz (ed.), *TV and Teens: Experts Look at the Issues*. Reading, Mass.: Addison-Wesley.

Roberts, E., D. Kline, and J. Gagnon (1978). *Family Life and Sexual Learning: A Study of the Role of Parents in the Sexual Learning of Children*. N.p.: Population Education.

Wartella, Ellen, ed. (1979). *Children Communicating: Media and Development of Thought, Speech, Understanding*. Beverly Hills, Calif.: Sage Publications, 286pp. (Sage Annual Reviews of Communication Research, Vol. 7).

Williams, F., R. LaRose, and F. Frost (1981). *Children, Television and Sex-Role Stereotyping*. New York: Praeger.

Journals

Bailyn, L. (1959). "Mass Media and Children: A Study of Exposure Habits and Cognitive Effects," *Psychological Monogram*, 73:1–48.

Beagles-Roos, J., and I. Gat (1983). "Specific Impact of Radio and Television on Children's Story Comprehension," *Journal of Educational Psychology*, 75:128–135.

Berry, Gordon L. (1977). "Television and the Urban Child: Some Educational Policy Implications," *Education and Urban Society*, Vol. 10, No. 1, pp. 31–54.

Bruyn, Henry B. (1978). "TV's Effect on Children: An Opinion Survey of Pediatricians," *Journal of School Health,* Vol. 48, No. 8, pp. 474–476.

Carrera, M. (1976). "Peer Group Sex Information and Education," *Journal of Research and Development in Education,* 10:1.

Christensen, P., P. DeBenedittes, and T. Lindloff (1985). "Children's Use of Audio Media." *Communication Research,* 12, 3:327–343.

Cobb, N.J., J. Stevens-Long, and S. Goldstein (1982). "The Influence of Televised Models on Toy Preference in Children." *Sex Roles,* 8, 10:1075–1080.

DePietro, R., and R.L. Allen (1984). "Adolescents' Communication Styles and Learning About Birth Control," *Adolescence,* 19, 76:827–837.

Dickinson, G. (1978). "Adolescent Sex Information Sources: 1964–1974," *Adolescence,* 13, 52:653–658.

DiGiovanni, C., and F. Polk (1986). "Adolescents Must Be Taught About Threats of AIDS," *Second Opinion,* 41231–41286.

Durkin, Kevin (1984). "Children's Account of Sex-Role Stereotypes in Television," *Communication Research,* 11, 3(July):341–362.

Durkin, Kevin (1985). "Television Sex-Role Acquisition I: Content," *British Journal of Social Psychology,* 24:101–113.

Eisenstock, B. (1984). "Sex Role Differences in Children's Identification with Counterstereotypical Television Portrayals," *Sex Roles,* 10:417–430.

Further Reading

Greenson, L.E. (1986). "Discussion of Media Influences and Other Selected Issues in Adolescent Psychology Texts," *American Psychologist,* 41:1385–1386.

Hansen, Christie H., and Ranald D. Hansen (1988). "How Rock Music Videos Can Change What Is Seen When Boy Meets Girl: Priming Stereotypic Appraisal of Social Interactions," *Sex Roles,* 10:417–430.

Heinz, J. (1983). "National Leadership for Children's Television," *American Psychologist,* 38:317–319.

Jorgensen, S.R. (1981). "Sex Education and the Reduction of Adolescent Pregnancies: Prospects for the 1980s," *Journal of Early Adolescence,* 1:38–52.

Klapper, H. (1978). "Childhood Socialization and Television," *Public Opinion Quarterly,* 42, 3:426–430.

Larson, R., and R. Kubey (1983). "Television and Music: Contrasting Media in Adolescent Life," *Youth and Society,* 15, 1:13–31.

Leming, James S. (1978). "Rock Music and the Socialization of Moral Values in Early Adolescence," *Youth and Society,* 14, 4(June):363–383.

O'Bryant, S., and C. Couder-Bolz (1978). "The Effects of Television on Children's Stereotyping of Women's Work Roles," *Journal of Vocational Behavior,* 12:233–244.

Pingree, S. (1978). "The Effects of Non-Sexist Television Commercials and Perceptions of Reality on Children's Attitudes About Women," *Psychology of Women Quarterly,* 2:262–276.

Rosenbaum, J., and L. Prinsky (1987). "Sex, Violence and Rock 'n' Roll: Youth's Perception of Popular Music," *Popular Music and Society,* 11 (Summer).

Rossiter, John R. (1977). "Reliability of a Short Test Measuring Children's Attitudes Toward TV Commercials," *Journal of Consumer Research,* Vol. 3, No. 4, pp. 179–184.

Rothschild, Nancy, and Michael Morgan (1987). "Cohesion and Control: Adolescents' Relationships with Parents as Mediators of Television," *Journal of Early Adolescence,* 7, 3:299–314.

Rubinstein, E.I. (1983). "Television and Behavior: Research Conclusion of the 1982 NIMH Report and Their Policy Implications," *American Psychologist,* 38:820–825.

Safran, Claire (1979). "What Parents Say About Children's TV," *Redbook* (October), Vol. 153, pp. 50, 155–158, 162.

Seltzer, S. (1976). "Quo Vadis, Baby?: Changing Adolescent Values as Reflected in the Lyrics of Popular Music," *Adolescence,* 11:419–429.

Spanier, G.B. (1977). "Sources of Sex Information and Pre-Marital Sex Behavior," *Journal of Sex Research,* 13, 2:73–88.

Surlin, Stuart H., and Joseph Domonick (1970–71). "TV's Function as a Third Parent for Black and White Teen-Agers," *Journal of Broadcasting* (Winter), 15:55–63.

Udrey, J.R., et al. (1972). "Can Mass Media Advertising Increase Contraceptive Use?" *Family Planning Perspectives,* 4:37.

Conference Papers and Project Reports

Anderson, Daniel R. (1979). "Active and Passive Processes in Children's Television Viewing." (Paper presented at the Annual Meeting of the American Psychological Association — 87th, New York, N.Y., September 1–5) 24pp.

Banks, Seymour, and Rajinder Gupta (1979). "Television as a Dependent Variable, for a Change." (Paper presented at the Annual Meeting of the American Psychological Association — 87th, New York, N.Y., September 1–5) 21pp.

Comstock, George, and Robin E. Cobbey (1978). "Television and the Children of Ethnic Minorities." (Paper presented at the Annual Meeting of the Association for Education in Journalism — 61st, Seattle, Wash., August 13–16) 30pp.

Greenberg, B.S., R.L. Linsangan, A. Soderman, et al. (1987). "Adolescents and Their Exposure to Television and Movie Sex." Project Report #4, Michigan State: Dept. of Telecommunication.

Greenberg, B.S., M. Siemicki, S. Dorfman, et al. (1986). "Sex Content in R-rated Films Viewed by Adolescents." Project CAST Report #3, Michigan State: Dept. of Telecommunication.

Greenberg, B.S., C. Stanley, M. Siemicki, et al. (1986). "Sex Content on Soaps and Primetime Series Most Viewed by Adolescents." Project CAST Report #2, Michigan State: Dept. of Telecommunication.

Kimball, M.M. (1977). "Television and Children's Sex-Role Attitudes," in T.M. Williams (chair). "The Impact of Television: A Natural Experiment Involving Three Communities." Symposium at Meeting of the Canadian Psychological Association, Vancouver.

Waite, B.M., and M.A. Paludi (1987). "Sex-Role Stereotyping in Popular Music Videos." Presented at the meeting of the Midwestern Psychological Association, Chicago.

Newspapers and Periodicals

Collins, G. (1987). "AIDS and TV: What to Tell a Young Child." *The New York Times* (March 9): Style Section.

Cromelin, Richard (1987). "Parents Get the Message from Video," *Los Angeles Times,* August 22.

Du Brow, Rick (1987). "Moral Dilemma on the Airwaves," *Los Angeles Herald Examiner,* Sunday, February 15.

Harmetz, Aljean (1987). "Films from Hollywood Enter the AIDS Era," *The New York Times* (Arts/Entertainment), Thursday, June 25.

Ingrassia, Michele, and Nicholas Golberg (1987). "Teen-agers and Sex: The Influence of Popular Culture (Mixed Messages)," *Newsday,* Wednesday, June 24.

Lambert, B. (1988). "Flood of Phone Calls on AIDS Tied to Mailing," *New York Times* (July 3):12.

Lewin, Tamar (1987). "New Sex Mores Are Chilling TV Ardor," *The New York Times* (Arts & Leisure), Sunday, March 8.

Mehren, Elizabeth (1988). "New Study Claims TV Fails to Balance Sex, Responsibility," *Los Angeles Times,* Wednesday, January 27.

Shales, Tom (1988). "'Love' Is Bleech," *Washington Post,* April 1.

Sterritt, David (1987). "Off Broadway Play 'Beirut' Imagines a Special AIDS Dilemma," *The Christian Science Monitor,* Wednesday, June 24.

Unger, Arthur (1987). "'An Enemy Among Us' Tackles a Difficult Theme," *The Christian Science Monitor,* Tuesday, July 21.

Other Publications

Fromm, M.L. (1981). "The Effects of Music Upon the Values of Complaint and Non-Complaint Adolescents." (Ph.D. Dissertation, University of Colorado at Boulder.)

Planned Parenthood Federation of America (1987). "American Teenagers Speak: Sex, Myth, TV and Birth Control." New York: PPFA.

Silverman, L.T., and J.N. Sprafkin (1980). "Adolescents' Reacting to Televised Sexual Innuendos." New York: American Broadcasting Co. (April).

TV Viewer (1980). "Impact of TV on Adolescent Girls' Sexual Attitudes and Behavior." 13(Feb. 14):1–2.

INDEX

Numbers refer to entries, not to pages.

Abortion 35, 82, 210, 211, 213
Abramson, P.R. 44
Adams, Bonnie 174
Advertising 7, 13, 18, 20, 39, 66, 90, 115, 145, 151, 194, 211
AIDS 54, 69, 191, 195, 196, 208, 209, 216, 217, 222, 225
AIDS International 228
Alan Guttmacher Institute 229
American Alliance Publications 230
American Association of Sex Educators, Counselors and Therapists (AASECT) 231
American Citizens Concerned for Life Education Fund 232
American College Health Association 233
American Educational Films 234
American Psychological Association 87, 134, 140, 166, 170, 198
American Red Cross AIDS Education Office 235
American Social Health Association (ASHA) 236
Amoroso, Donald M. 125
Association of Childhood Education International 237
Atkin, Charles K. 148
Avery, Robert K. 45

Bandura, Albert 46
Banks, Ivan W. 47
Baran, Stanley J. 2, 121, 122
Barcus, F. Earle 3
Barrow, Austin E. 4
Bell, Daniel 8
Bell, Norma 17, 72
Birth Control *see* Contraception
Blacks 47, 83, 131, 176
Blackside Films 238
Blanchard-Fields, Fredda 60, 123
Bloomfield, Kim A. 124
Body Awareness Resource Network (BARN) 68
Bosworth, Kris 68
Brion-Meisels, Stevens 49
Brislin-Slutz, Jo Ann 85, 168
Brodie, Mollyann 150
Brown, J.D. 12, 166
Brown, Jane 51, 129
Brown, Marvin 125
Bruzzant, Liza 150
Busby, Linda 5, 6

Cambridge Documentary Films 239
Cantor, Joel M. 50, 126
Cantor, Muriel G. 50, 126
The Center for Disease Control 240

Index

The Center for Early Adolescence 100, 241

Center for Population Options 1, 15, 19, 65, 75, 109, 112, 116, 118, 120, 124, 128, 133, 158, 182, 190, 191, 194, 195, 216, 223, 224, 242

Center for Research and Education in Sexuality 243

Center for Research on the Influence of Television on Children 244

Center for the Study of Child and Adolescent Development 245

Chamberlin, Leslie J. 127

Chambers, Norman 127

Chelter, Mary K. 100

Chewning, Betty 68

Child Welfare League of America, Inc. 246

Childers, Kim Walsh 51, 128, 129, 192

Children's books 61, 144

Children's Defense Fund 67, 247

Churches 132, 141, 181

The Cinema 45, 47, 121, 151, 174

Claussenius, David 76, 159, 207

Comstock, G. 131

Concerned Women of America 248

Contraception 44, 47, 57, 58, 59, 63, 76, 81, 82, 89, 128, 136, 159, 171, 194, 197, 199, 200, 202, 203, 204, 206, 207, 211, 213, 214, 215, 218, 220, 225

Coon, Robert 123

Corder-Bolz, Charles R. 83

Cordua, Glenn 10

Counseling 68

Counseling and Personnel Services Clearinghouse 249

Courtney, Alice E. 7

Csikszentmihalyi, Mihaly 52

Cullari, Salvatore 53, 132

Dambrot, Faye H. 8

Day, Patricia M. 68

Derfler, Richard 174

Desmond, Sharon 217

DiClemente, Ralph J. 54, 196

Documents Associates 250

Dohrmann, Rita 9

Drabman, Ronald S. 10

Dryfoos, Loy A. 197

Duncan, David F. 55

Durall, Jean A. 11

Education, Training and Research Associates 251

Ehrenberg, Mariam 56

Ehrenberg, Otto 56

Eisen, Marvin 57, 134, 198

Encyclopaedia Britannica Educational Corp 252

Entertainment Industry Coalition on AIDS 253

Faber, R.J. 12

The Family 24, 56, 64, 89, 94, 96, 99, 104, 137, 138, 139, 140, 171, 201

Family Life Information Exchange 254

Fernandez-Collado, C.F. 135, 145, 148

Film and Television Documentation Center 255

Films see The Cinema

Films Inc. 256

Fink, Mitchell 58

Finkel, David J. 59, 136, 199

Finkel, Madelon L. 59, 136, 199

Fisher, Terri D. 137, 138, 139, 140

Foltz, K. 200

Ford Foundation 257

Fouhy, Beth 142

Franzblau, Susan 143
Friedman, Leslie J. 13
Frueh, Terry 19, 23, 60, 80
Fuchs, Lucy 61, 144
Furstenberg, F.F. 86, 170

Gagnon, J. 96
Garwood, Patricia 152
Gay Men's Health Crisis 258
Gays 35
Gerbner, George 62
Gerrard, Meg 63, 202
Gibbens, Frederick X. 63, 202
Gibbs, Margaret 174
The Gifted 37
Gikonyo, Waithira Lucy 201
Goldfarb, Lori 63, 202
Goldstein, Cynthia 203
Gore, Tipper 64
Graef, D. 145, 148
Greenberg, B.S. 135, 145, 146, 147, 148, 149
Greenfield, Patricia M. 150
Guidance Associates 259
Gustafson, David H. 68

Haffner, Debra W. 66, 151
Haignere, Clara S. 67, 204
Hajcak, Frank 152
Hammer, David 10
Hansen, Christine 16, 153
Hansen, Ronald D. 16, 153
Harvey, Philip D. 76, 159, 207
Hawkins, Robert P. 68
Health Belief Model (HBM) 57, 134, 198
Heeter, Carrie 147, 149
Heffley, Lynne 69
Hein, K. 70
Hendry, Leo B. 71
Herx, Elicia J. 172, 218

Himmelweit, Hilde T. 17, 72
Holroyd, H.J. 73
Homosexuality *see* Gays
Horn, John 74, 154, 205

Jarvie, Gregory J. 10
Jeffries, Georgia 206
Johnson, D.K. 18
Judge Baker Guidance Center 49

Kaw Valley Films & Video, Inc. 260
Kellan, Jeff 154
Kelley, Kathryn 156
Kelly, Marcy 66, 151
The Kids on the Block, Inc. 261
Kingsdale, David 150
Kinsey Institute for Research in Sex, Gender, and Reproduction 262
Kippax, Susan 164
Kirby, Douglas 76, 159, 207
Kline, D. 96
Koop, C. Everett 208
Korzenny, Felipe 148
Koyamatsu, Kristi 150
Kukulka, Gary 217

Laboratory for the Study of Adolescence 263
Lake, Sara 160
Lauer, Rachel M. 20
Learning Corporation of America 264
Levy, Joseph R. 77
Lewter, Dean Worth 209
Liebert, Robert M. 161
Linsangan, M. 147
Linsangan, Renato 149

Index

Lopate, Carol 21
Lopez-Johnson, Pam 78
Louis Harris and Associates 22, 210
Luria, Zella 79

McDowell, Eugene E. 37
McGhee, Paul E. 14, 23, 60, 80
McGraw-Hill Films 265
McLeod, J.M. 12
Madonna 41, 73
Magazines *see* Periodicals
Masland, Jonathan L. 188
Mathews, Robert 123
Mechanic, M.B. 44
Media Action Research Center (MARC) 266
Meyer, Buf 24
Meyer, Manfred 25, 81, 162, 212
Meyers, Renee 4
Mikus, Robert 53, 132
Miles, Beth 26
Moore, K.A. 86, 170
Morgan, Michael 27, 163
Morgan, Michael Jay 28
Movies *see* The Cinema
Mullis, Ronald L. 99, 173
Musialowski, Donna 156
Murphy, Mary 4
Murray, John P. 164
Music Videos 16, 48, 73, 87, 123, 150, 155, 169, 180, 224

National Association of Broadcasters 130
National Association of Television Program Executives 62
National Council of the Churches of Christ 187
National Family Planning and

Reproductive Health Association, Inc. 267
National Institute of Mental Health 165
National Public Radio 268
Neal, James A. 85, 168
Network Publications 269
New Day Films 270
Newcomer, Susan F. 82, 166, 213
Nissen, Ursula 25, 81, 162, 212
Nixon, Karen 150
Novar, Marty 76, 159, 207

O'Bryant, Shirley L. 83
O'Keeffe, Barbara J. 4
O'Kelly, Charlotte G. 29
Okigbo, Charles 84
Ornelas, Kriemhild, Conee 30, 167

Padgett, Vernon R. 85, 168
Patrick, Helen 71
Patterson, Jana N. 10
Periodicals 47, 48, 117, 118, 189
Perennial Education, Inc. 272
Peterson, Dena L. 169
Peterson, J. 86, 170
Peterson, R. 48
Pfost, Karen S. 169
Planned Parenthood Federation of America, Inc. 22, 67, 82, 88, 89, 171, 204, 210, 211, 213, 214, 215, 273
Plante, Thomas 63, 202
Pornography 55, 79, 125, 168
Pregnancy 178, 197, 204, 205, 206, 210, 214, 221, 224
Price, James H. 90, 217
Project Respect 274
Project SHARE 275
Prostitution 34, 35

Index

Public Broadcasting Service 276
Puttman, David 92
Pyramid Film & Video 277

Radio 47, 151, 224
Rape 34, 35, 178, 221
Raskin, Alex 93
Reep, Diana C. 8
Reeves, Byron 114, 146
Reis, Janet 172, 218
Rensberger, Boyce 94
Rifkin, Ira 95
Roberts, E. 96
Roberts, Elizabeth J. 97
Robertson, Stephen J. 10
Rubin, Alan 98
Rubinstein, Eli A. 32, 35, 143, 176

San Francisco AIDS Foundation 278
Sanders, Gregory F. 99, 173
Satow, K. 18
Scalrs, Peter 100
Schwartz, Meg 101, 219
Schyller, Ingela 102
Search Institute 279
Sederman, A. 147
Seiter, Ellen 103
Serbin, Lias A. 36
Sex Education 58, 67, 82, 89, 94, 100, 204, 210, 211, 213, 215
Sex Education Coalition 280
Sex Information and Education Council of the US (SIECUS) 66, 151, 281
Sexism 29, 32, 40, 176
Sexual Activity 2, 27, 49, 58, 67, 70, 87, 101, 110, 122, 136, 140, 152, 185, 188, 204, 205, 206
Sexually Transmitted Diseases (STD) 67, 204, 210, 211, 219

Shapiro, C.H. 104
Siemicki, M. 147
Sigal, Janet 174
Signorielli, Nancy 31, 175
Silverman, L. Theresa 32, 34, 35, 176
Simon, Rogers 33, 177, 220
Singer, Dorothy G. and Jerome L. 105
Sipes, Sherri 178, 221
Skorlich, Kerry 179
Smothers, J. 106
Soap Operas 21, 30, 50, 77, 107, 128, 147, 149, 167, 178, 221
Society for the Scientific Study of Sex 282
Soderman, Anne 149
Sprafkin, Joyce N. 32, 34, 35, 143, 161, 176
Stanley, C. 147
Stauloff, Wendy 150
Steinbrook, Robert 222
Sternglaz, Sarah Hall 36
Stewart, Cyrus S. 185, 186
Stillion, Judith M. 37
Stone, Rebecca 223
Strasburger, Victor C. 107
Streenland, Sally 38, 108
Strover, Sharon 180
Sunburst Communications 283
Swanson, David L. 4

Tan, Alexis S. 39
Television 2, 3, 4, 5, 6, 8, 9, 11, 12, 14, 15, 17, 18, 19, 22, 23, 25, 26, 27, 28, 31, 32, 33, 34, 35, 36, 38, 40, 42, 43, 47, 51, 52, 58, 62, 67, 71, 72, 73, 74, 78, 81, 86, 87, 90, 95, 96, 97, 98, 101, 102, 103, 105, 107, 109, 112, 113, 116, 119, 120, 121, 122, 123, 124, 127, 130, 131, 135, 142, 143, 145, 146, 148, 149, 151, 158, 160,

137

Index

161, 162, 163, 164, 165, 166, 170, 176, 177, 205, 206, 211, 212, 219, 220, 224
Temoshok, Lydia 54, 196
Thompson, Cynthia 142
Thornburg, Hershel D. 110, 111
Truglio, Rosemarie 112, 182
Tumulty, Karen 225

Udry, Richard J. 183
United Nations 226
US Department of Health and Human Services 271
US Public Health Service 284
United States Senate 227
Uselding, Douglas K. 40

Van Hoose, John H. 113, 184

Vener, Arthur M. 185, 186
Violence 35, 44, 187

Walters, Richard H. 46
Ware, Edward 125
Wartella, Ellen 114
Waszak, Cynthia 223
Weaver, James B. 188
Werkman, Diana L. 124
Whipple, Thomas W. 7
White, Barbie 117, 189
Wilson, Patricia I. 47
Winship, Elizabeth 118, 190
Women's AIDS Project 285
Workman, Diana 119

Zellman, Gail L. 57, 134, 198
Zillman, Dolf 188
Zorn, Jim 54, 196